Christina Murphy

Texas Christian University

Workbook

The Prentice Hall Guide for
College Writers

Stephen Reid

Colorado State University

PRENTICE HALL, Englewood Cliffs, New Jersey 078632

Editorial/production supervision and
  interior design: *John A. Nestor*
Manufacturing buyer: *Laura Crossland*

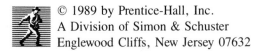
Printed in the United States of America

10 9 8 7 6 5 4 3 2 1

ISBN 0-13-150152-6

Prentice-Hall International (UK) Limited, *London*
Prentice-Hall of Australia Pty. Limited, *Sydney*
Prentice-Hall Canada Inc., *Toronto*
Prentice-Hall Hispanoamericana, S.A., *Mexico*
Prentice-Hall of India Private Limited, *New Delhi*
Prentice-Hall of Japan, Inc., *Tokyo*
Simon & Schuster Asia Pte. Ltd., *Singapore*
Editora Prentice-Hall do Brasil, Ltda., *Rio de Janeiro*

TABLE OF CONTENTS

WORKBOOK (wurk' book) n. 1. A booklet containing problems and exercises in which a student may directly write, calculate, or the like. 2. A manual containing operating instructions. 3. A book in which a record is kept of work proposed or accomplished.

NOTE TO THE STUDENT

A workbook asks that you work at, practice, apply the concepts you are learning in your composition class. One concept is the writing process itself, the various stages of thinking, creating, organizing, and editing that result in the art of writing well.

Writing well is not so much a difficult task as it is one that requires motivation, self-discipline, and the type of sustained effort to improve known as "practice." Your workbook provides you with a series of guided exercises or "practices" that will help you teach yourself a great deal about writing well.

The focus of the exercises is upon critical thinking, or the type of in-depth analytical and creative thinking involved in expressing one's ideas. Critical thinking is the core of the writing process because critical thinking enables you to reflect upon, consider, and develop your ideas. Without ideas, you would be unable to write, for there would be nothing for you to communicate. With ideas, you are motivated and challenged to write, and writing itself becomes an easier process. Critically well-conceived thought will enable you to formulate the ideas you wish to communicate, as well as to develop the organizational strategies that needed to make your ideas clear to others.

Critical thinking (which also involves thoughtful reflection upon your writing processes), organization, style, and effective proofreading and editing make up the writing process. Your workbook will focus your attention on each aspect of this process, as well as suggest ways to use your own imagination and creativity to write effectively. Mastery of the writing process will come through understanding and practice, and mostly through a great deal of sustained effort. In your effort to become a better writer, think of your workbook as a helpful ally and your personal dedication and commitment to improving your skills as your greatest assets.

NOTE TO THE INSTRUCTOR

A workbook provides the student with opportunities for self-directed and self-paced learning to complement the instruction the student receives in the classroom and from the textbook. The focus of this workbook is upon critical thinking, or the type of reflective, well-considered, creative analysis necessary for a student to experience in order to express ideas clearly in writing. The premise of this workbook is that clear, in-depth thinking both generates and drives the writing process, and that to improve the clarity of a student's thinking greatly improves the quality of that student's writing.

The workbook is composed of a series of exercises or practices that guide the student in learning the analytical skills required in assessing topics and in responding to the issues these topics raise. The direction of the workbook is to involve the student in language and communication study in such a way that significant thinking occurs. In addition to an emphasis upon critical thinking, specific attention is directed to all aspects of the writing process concerned with organization, style, revision, proofreading and editing, so that the student can master the techniques involved in writing well.

The workbook exercises in critical thinking are presented as a series of heuristics, or questions directed toward having the student think about and assess an issue from a number of perspectives. The heuristics are directed or guided learning experiences in that each of the questions involved in the heuristic is intended to have the student think more fully upon a particular topic and consider, in general, the process of how one comes up with and evaluates ideas.

The heuristics emphasize for the student: (1) that the basic and most essential process of composition is discovery, or the creation, development, and refinement of one's ideas; and (2) that the knowledge necessary for producing writing of quality can be acquired through conscious, directed actions. For many students, for whom the writing process has seemed a complex, confusing, indecipherable, and profoundly difficult event, this realization that the writing process can be learned is a very freeing one.

For the instructor, the design of the workbook provides exercises that emphasize the techniques of successful writers, as well as topics and writing assignments to stimulate the student's creative process. The workbook is keyed to the chapters of the textbook, emphasizing material covered in the text and presenting writing assignments based upon issues generated by the text. In each chapter of the workbook, both individual and group exercises are presented, with the majority of the exercises functioning equally as well as either in-class or out-of-class writing assignments.

In providing exercises for critical thinking, this workbook focuses upon the cognitive skills involved in analytical thought, such as selecting, refining, and developing ideas; categorizing, comparing, and contrasting the issues presented by ideas; examining arguments and assumptions; reaching and evaluating inferences and deductions; and generating broad patterns of synthesis from given or inferred data. In this fashion, the critical thinking exercises in this workbook serve as prompts or catalysts for creative, in-depth thinking, which emphasizes the originality to develop new ideas; the flexibility to think of many kinds of ideas; and the ability to elaborate, or to think in terms of detailed ideas. Again the focus of the workbook is upon demystifying the creative process for students and presenting it as a way of thinking and problem solving that can be studied and learned.

A substantial number of the exercises are imbedded within the text of the workbook rather than listed numerically at the end of each chapter, which is the more common practice. This method of imbedding the exercises within the text of each chapter has been chosen because it encourages the student to read the material surrounding the exercises and thus have a clearer idea of what they are being asked to do in each exercise.

In this fashion, the student is introduced to important ideas raised by the text, as well as instructed in the requirements of each exercise. The assumption here is that allowing the student to perceive the exercise within the context of the issues raised by each chapter enables the exercises to have a more immediate and important role within the student's developing thinking processes than simply listing the exercises at the end as if they were incidental to the learning processes advocated by the chapter.

To foster the advancement of a student's capacity for critical and creative thinking, a number of the exercises in the workbook also focus upon antiphonal thinking, or the type of thought involved in considering challenges to primary ideas or assumptions. In a number of instances, especially in the Point/Counterpoint sections, students are asked to reflect upon issues raised in the textbook and to consider and evaluate the premises underlying these concepts. The student is taught to evaluate ideas and to assess their merit, rather than to take all ideas as inherently valid and correct simply because they have been articulated with some measure of detail. One assumption is that this model of thinking best mirrors the type of problem solving skills students will be expected to manifest as an intellectual ability throughout their lives. Instructing students early in this method of thinking enhances their opportunities for personal enrichment and for future academic and professional success.

In its fullest dimension, this workbook is designed to produce for the student a dynamic interaction amongst the learning experiences provided by the composition instructor and by the textbook. The tone of the workbook is dialogic and personal, rather than directional and impersonal. Conversational passages encourage both understanding and application of concepts, versus the more conventional approach of structuring a workbook as a series of directives, absolutes, and fill in the blanks exercises. While many workbooks instruct students in the writing process by providing a series of drills or repetitive exercises, this workbook seeks from the student an active intellectual engagement in the process of learning to write well by understanding and applying the type of in-depth critical thinking involved in the clear expression of one's ideas. To this extent, the workbook borrows from Aristotle the idea that good writing consists of clear ideas well expressed, while emphasizing for the student the intricate relationship between language and thought as the essence of writing well.

"IN CREATING, THE HARDEST THING'S TO BEGIN"

--JAMES RUSSELL LOWELL

INSTRUCTIONS FOR USING THE WORKBOOK

Each of the exercises that follows is presented as a set of interrelated questions. The questions are designed to set you to thinking about the implications of a particular topic or writing assignment. In this way, the questions are an exercise in critical thinking and in problem solving because the questions in each exercise will help you come up with ideas, select and analyze your ideas in terms of a meaningful organizational strategy, and elaborate your ideas into a completed essay.

Often, for many writers, the hardest part of writing is knowing where to begin in order to come up with something to say, and each of these exercises is designed to meet this difficulty head on by offering a type of guided thinking exercise that will show you how to look at a writing assignment from a number of perspectives.

In working on these exercises, consider each set of questions as a whole, not as individual questions that should be answered individually. The questions are designed to prompt and stimulate your own creative processes. And, because the questions function as a whole, each question provides another puzzle piece, another perspective, upon the problem of completing the writing assignment at hand.

Followed correctly and used to stimulate your own thinking, the questions will help you shape in your own mind an approach to the writing assignment. Thus, it is extremely important that you look upon each set of questions as a unit or as a unified thinking exercise that is leading you toward the formulation of your own essay response.

Do not attempt to respond to the questions by answering each one in an individual and sequential fashion. In other words, given a certain number of questions in a set, do not answer question number one, then number two, then three, and so forth. This will defeat the purpose of the exercise and will lead to some rather ineffective and boring writing. Instead, use the questions to begin your own creative thinking about the topic, and then begin to express in writing the ideas that have come to your mind.

At first, you will have a natural tendency to want to answer each question individually. This is a predictable response, since we are used to following orders and following orders in a sequence. It may be hard for you to take in all the information that each set of questions provides, and you may feel overwhelmed.

Be patient. Soon you will begin to grasp the idea that the questions are like having another "voice" or questioner in your head that is asking you exactly the type of questions you need to think about in order to do the assignment well. When this happens, the questions will seem less like separate and unrelated ideas and more like a carefully constructed exercise in the process of discovering your own creative ideas and insights.

While your teacher will have the final say on how long each of these writing assignments is to be, it will be to your advantage in improving your skills as a writer to think of answering each of these exercises in the length of at least one typed page, or about two hundred and fifty words. Anything less, say a short paragraph or two, and you might have a tendency to skim the surface of your ideas and to produce a fairly superficial essay. Anything much longer, and you might become repetitive and long-winded.

What is more important than the precise length of your essay, though, is your commitment to delving into the topic and trying to see it from a number of perspectives. This is the essence of creative thinking and of problem solving, for rarely do we encounter an important issue or problem that does not require that we consider the issue from a number of angles before deciding what to do. This factor will be especially important in the Point/Counterpoint sections, in which you will be asked to consider opposing arguments for issues and ideas raised by both your textbook and your workbook. Think of each writing assignment you are given as an intellectual problem, a challenge to be solved, and you will be aware of how a carefully constructed approach of thinking through the ideas involved in the assignment will help you become a better and more confident writer.

"IN ONESELF LIES THE WHOLE WORLD, AND IF YOU KNOW HOW TO LOOK AND LEARN, THEN THE DOOR IS THERE AND THE KEY IS IN YOUR HAND. NOBODY ON EARTH CAN GIVE YOU EITHER THAT KEY OR THE DOOR TO OPEN, EXCEPT YOURSELF."

--J. KRISHNAMURTI

CAUTION: **THIS WORKBOOK MAY CAUSE YOU TO THINK!**

"INSIDE THE PENCIL CROUCH WORDS

THAT HAVE NEVER BEEN WRITTEN"

--W.S. MERWIN

1

CHAPTER ONE: MYTHS AND RITUALS

Here is everything you need for writing well:

abcdefghijklmnopqrstuvwxyz

1234567890

, ; : . ! ? ' " -- / ( ) [ ]

Well, actually, there is one thing missing: you. Or, more precisely, your imagination and creativity, for one truth of the writing process is that each writer begins with the same twenty-six letters, the same nine digits, and the same handful of punctuation marks, and the only thing that separates one writer from the next is the way that he or she chooses to put these letters, these numbers, these punctuation marks together in order to create meaningful statements to share with others.

No one can say exactly how your imaginative, creative process will work; no one can know precisely the ideas your mind will formulate. All that can be said is that the ideas you develop will be unique, the result of your own particular experience of the world. Therefore, your creative process (your mind and how it works), should be a source of wonder and fascination for you, and learning to understand your own thinking processes should enable you to think with even greater depth and clarity. Some ideas associated with the concept of *thinking* are: to form an idea in the mind; to have a thought; to reason about, reflect upon, or ponder; to decide; to judge or regard; to believe or suppose; to expect, anticipate, or hope; to remember, call to mind; or imagine; to visualize; to exercise the power of reason; to draw inferences and make judgments; to weigh something carefully; to contemplate.

Mind yields this type of definition: the principle of intelligence; the spirit of consciousness regarded as an aspect of reality; the sum total of of all of a person's conscious states, including thoughts, memories, feelings, and emotions.

An interesting and very true fact about consciousness, intelligence, creativity, and insight is that none of these faculties of intellect is of any value without one simple factor, and that is *application*. It matters not how brilliant you are if you do not apply your brilliance through hard work and diligent application. You might wonder why your workbook is weighted so heavily toward exercises that call upon you to *apply* your knowledge rather than just accumulate a great deal of information about writing and store it for future use. Three reasons: (1) learning works best when it involves action, personal commitment, and personal investment; (2) talents not used and developed through practice can decline and be wasted or lost; and (3) talents worked at, developed, practiced and nurtured can intensify and lead to the acquisition of even greater talents and abilities. The key word here is *motivation*, and that is an intangible personal characteristic that only you can bring to your efforts to improve your skills as a writer.

An illustration of this principle is contained in the autobiography of Benjamin Franklin, a self-taught philosopher, historian, inventor, essayist, and philanthropist who became one of America's most important political figures during the Revolutionary period. In this selection [from L. Jesse Lemisch's *Benjamin Franklin: The Autobiography and Other Writings*], Franklin discusses how he came to be a better writer once he realized that the skills he possessed were not adequate to his purposes. In a debate with his friend Collin, Franklin Franklin quickly came to realize that his adversary was a much more skilled rhetorician than he. As a result, Franklin set about on a course of self-improvement to see how he could become a more eloquent writer. He describes the process in this fashion:

[Collin] was naturally more eloquent, having a greater plenty of words, and sometimes, as I thought, I was vanquished more by his fluency than by the strength of his reasons. As we parted without settling the point . . . I sat down to put my arguments in writing . . . . Three or four letters on a side had passed, when my father happened to find my papers and read them. Without entering into the subject in dispute, he took occasion to talk with me about my manner of writing, observed that though I had the advantage of my antagonist in correct spelling and pointing [punctuation] . . . I fell far short in elegance of expression, in method and in perspicuity--of which he convinced me by several instances. I saw the justice of his remarks and thence grew more attentive to my manner of writing, and determined to endeavor to improve my style.

About this time I met with an odd volume of the *Spectator*. I bought it, read it over and over, and was much delighted with it. I thought the writing excellent and wished if possible to imitate it. With that view, I took some of the papers, and making short hints of the sentiment in each sentence, laid them by a few days, and then without looking at the book, tried to complete the papers again by expressing each hinted sentiment at length and as fully as it had been expressed before, in any suitable words that should occur to me. Then I compared my *Spectator* with the original, discovered some of my faults, and corrected them. But I found I wanted a stock of words or a readiness in recollecting and using them, which I thought I should have acquired before that time if I had gone on making verses; since the continual search for words of the same import but of different length to suit the measure, or of different sound for the rhyme would have laid me under a constant necessity of searching for variety, and also have tended to fix that variety in my mind, and make me master of it. Therefore, I took some of the tales in the *Spectator* and turned them into verse, and after a time, when I had pretty well forgotten the prose, turned them back again. I also sometimes jumbled my collection of hints into confusion, and after some weeks endeavored to reduce them into the best order before I began to form the full sentences and complete the paper. This was to teach me method in the arrangement of the thoughts. By comparing my work afterwards with the original, I discovered many faults and corrected them; but I sometimes had the pleasure of fancying that in certain particulars of small import I had been lucky enough to improve the method or the language, and this encouraged me to think that I might possibly in time come to be a tolerable English writer, of which I was extremely ambitious.

Franklin's account illustrates some important ideas about improving one's skills as a writer. First, Franklin's dedication and motivation are apparent. He had a reason, a desire, and an impetus [in the *Spectator*] to improve his ability to communicate effectively and to be more persuasive with his writing. Second, we see his consciousness on display here, the particular and unique way his mind came up with ideas to write about and found rhetorical structures appropriate to the expression of his thoughts. He exemplified in his search important ideas about consciousness and creativity and about how intellect (mind) and language intersect in the acts of thinking and writing to create meaning.

All ideas about thinking and the mind reveal how complex and unique each person's consciousness is as the source of all intellectual functioning and creativity. The chances are, though, that if you are like most people, you haven't given a great deal of thought to your own thinking and creative processes--at least enough thought to figure out if there is a pattern to your thinking and if that pattern can be improved upon and enhanced. This question forms an excellent starting point for your first writing/thinking exercise, which begins with a consideration of your own thought processes.

Exercise #1

How do you think? What is the usual way your mind operates? Do you notice details and small aspects first, or do you generally perceive large patterns and broad ideas? Do you often think about your own thinking, or do you consider it something you just do, like breathing? What are some of the hardest things for you to think about? What are some of the easiest? How difficult do you find it to think about thinking? In what ways do you think your thinking can be improved?

Let us start with the assumption that your thinking processes will be as unique as your writing myths and rituals. This is the snowflake theory applied to writing: no two writers think alike, and no two writers compose in exactly the same fashion. Interestingly, even though no two writers think or write in exactly the same way, nearly all beginning writers share the same myths about either (1) how difficult writing is, or (2) exactly how writing should be done.

A number of these myths arise from insecurity: "Writing is too difficult for me. It's too hard to learn. I've never been a good writer. I don't know where to begin. I hate writing because it's the only thing I've never been able to get very good at. All my other courses I can study and get A's in, but not writing."

A number of these myths are the result of misperceptions: "Writing is not an important skill in today's world anymore. We have other means of communicating with each other, like telephones and TV." When I get my first job, I won't need to write because I'll have a secretary who'll do it for me." Freshman English is the most unimportant course I'll ever take. They only require it because nobody would take it if they didn't have to." "Pretty soon they'll have computers that will fix everything for you in writing, so I don't have to learn all that unimportant, boring grammar stuff." "Writing is either something you can do or you can't. Some people are born able to write well, and I wasn't one of them."

An even greater number of these myths develop from misinformation: "There's only one correct way to write." "All good essays must have an introduction, three paragraphs of development, and a summary conclusion." "Never use *I* when you write." "An essay will only be good if you make an outline first." "Don't make any changes in your first draft; you'll ruin your creativity." "The only way to be a good writer is to be very hard on yourself for any mistakes you make." "Only poor writers need to revise their work."

Exercise #2

What are some of the myths you believe about writing? Are any of your myths misperceptions? How so?

Answering the second question in Exercise #2 might have been difficult, for it is often hard to know when we are perceiving anything correctly or incorrectly. Psychologists tell us that we are often ruled by perceptual bias, which means that people usually see what they expect to see--and ignore what they don't expect.

When students are learning to write, often they expect to see difficulties and problems, and often what they expect to see comes true. Perhaps approaching writing with an open mind, with no preconceptions, would free many students from this trap of predicting their own troubles with writing.

Thus, even though you might wonder why your textbook and your workbook are devoting entire chapters to the issues of the myths surrounding writing, you might also be coming to realize how importantly your views of writing will shape your outcomes. Believe that writing is a skill too difficult to learn, and you make writing too difficult to learn. Believe that writing, like any skill, can be learned and mastered through hard work, diligence, and patience, and you make writing learnable. That is

5

one of the reasons why both your textbook and your workbook encourage you to examine the myths you have lived by concerning writing.

Free Writing #1

Free write for ten or fifteen minutes on why you feel so many myths and misperceptions surround the writing process. Write freely, following the natural flow of your ideas, and do not stop the flow of your writing to correct, edit, or revise your work.

One of the major myths that surrounds the writing process is the tendency most beginning writers have of focusing upon the entire task of writing, which seems monumental and overwhelming, rather than breaking the task down into parts that are manageable and far less intimidating. Author Annie Dillard phrases this fear in this fashion: "You know when you think about writing a book, you think it is overwhelming. But, actually, you break it down into tiny little tasks any moron could do."

While Dillard's final statement is a bit of an exaggeration, her view overall demonstrates that breaking the task of writing into manageable segments is an important aspect of keeping the demands of writing assignments in perspective and overcoming the potential for writer's block. John Steinbeck, author of *The Grapes of Wrath*, discusses the issue in this manner in *Travels with Charlie*, in which he discusses his plans to tour the entire United States by truck.

And suddenly the United States became huge beyond belief and impossible ever to cross. I wondered how I'd got myself mixed up in a project that couldn't be carried out. It was like starting to write a novel. When I face the desolate impossibility of writing five hundred pages, a sick sense of failure falls on me, and I know I can never do it. This happens every time. Then gradually I write one page and then another. One day's work is all I can permit myself to contemplate, and I eliminate the possibility of ever finishing.

As Steinbeck's description indicates, panic or writer's anxiety can be a common experience, even for the most experienced and accomplished of writers. You can overcome your hesitation to write, however, in the same way Steinbeck suggests, by writing one word, one sentence, one page at a time. The important issue is *to begin*, for beginning will increase your confidence and each page word, each sentence you write will contribute to making your confidence in yourself as a writer grow.

In this overall process of examining the myths and misperceptions that surround your writing, you might find, too, that a number of your views of writing have changed over the years. And this result should be very encouraging for you because it shows that one's perceptions of writing generally change as one's life situations change. Early in your life, speech, not written communication, was your primary means of expressing yourself. Later, as you matured and entered the world of social interaction and of social discourse, you began to discover that writing serves a very important function in society. For centuries, writing has been the medium through which people have recorded their thoughts and preserved them over time. To enter into the world of social interaction is to enter into a world in which the ability to express one's thoughts clearly to others becomes a primary importance.

Perhaps you don't believe this is true. Would you be willing to try an experiment to see? In fact, let's structure this as a Group Exercise, in which the class will need to participate as a whole.

Group Exercise #1

One person will be selected by the teacher or the class as the message giver (MG), whose responsibility it will be to bring to class a message of a moderate level of complexity and detail, such as one might find in a business memo, a sales brochure, or a newspaper or magazine article. The message should average around one hundred to one hundred and fifty words, and messages that include information on names, dates, places, and special events would be particularly valuable for this exercise.

The MG is also free to devise a message of his or her own and prepare it for the class. In this instance, typical messages prepared often read like business memos that indicate who will be meeting with whom, and when and where. Remember, though, for the purposes of the exercise, that the message should average between one hundred and one hundred and fifty words and should have a fairly complex level of details and specifics to it.

Examples of the types of messages that could be used in this exercise might include:

1). Opponents of the Morgan City Rapid Transit System have rejected Morgan City's plan for a $1 billion, 93-mile rail and downtown subway system designed to connect the suburbs with the downtown Central Business District (CBD). The group, led by former Morgan City mayor Milton "Bud" Gravely, said that the City Council needs to look carefully at its demographics for the suburbs, urging them to be aware that population growth in the suburbs has exceeded estimates for the past ten years by nearly 27%. The City Council's figures indicate a much slower rate of growth than what Gravely anticipates will be the case in the next fifteen years. Thus, the rapid transit system might be outdated before its construction is even completed and new revenue measures will have to be undertaken to bring the system in line with population needs and trends. Gravely urged acceptance of the Miller-Holzbein proposal, in which funding for the rapid transit system would be extended over a twenty-year period and financed, in part, from revenues from the new tollway that connects Morgan City with Cassaday County.

2). Thomas Rathway, Vice-President of Corporate Financing for Yates Microcomputer Systems, called on June 13th at 3:20 to ask that you meet with him at the Green Oaks Inn on Davis Avenue and Tarrant Boulevard on Monday, June 27th, at 8:30 a.m. He wants to discuss with you Yates's new proposal for combining semi-conductors with central processing units to increase the megabyte memory on the new Yates SR3000 series. He asked for your permission to bring Joe Henney, Comptroller and Chief Auditor, to the meeting to discuss possible contract options.

He also requested that you bring the file on the microcomputer system set up for the Gregory Wyndham account.

The MG will bring the message to class the day of the group exercise and not share it with anyone until the time comes. At this point, the class should separate itself from the MG, either by going outside the classroom and waiting in the hall, or by going to the back of the classroom so that conversation will not be overheard.

The MG will call one person forward, either from the back of the room or from outside in the hallway. The MG will let this first person read the message and take a few moments to absorb its details. Then the person who has read the message will tell what he or she can remember of the message to the next person in line.

The key idea here is that the first person will try to convey the message to the second person from memory only and will not share the written message with the second person at all. From this point on, the second person will tell the third person in line what he or she remembers of the message, and so on, until all the members in the class have had the message passed on to them.

When the message has completed its journey of repetitions and recountings, the last person to hear the message will tell the rest of the class what the message is. Comparisons will then be made between the original and the final messages.

Invariably, the messages will differ, and you may be amazed at the contrast between the two messages! Certainly, some of the content of the original message will have been lost. It's highly likely that some of the details of the message have been changed; it's even more probable that important details have been left out. In some instances you might discover that the two messages have very little to do with each other and that it is hard to believe that the second message is an outgrowth of the first.

It would be very difficult to run a business, or one's personal or professional life, with situations in which messages could change so dramatically within the space of a few minutes. And the situation becomes even more complicated as time passes. Imagine trying to reconstruct from memory the details of this message a day later, a month, or a year. It would be impossible. And remember this is only one message. Imagine trying to keep clear in your memory dozens of messages, perhaps hundreds, and you can begin to see how important writing becomes for preserving our ideas and enabling us to check the accuracy of what has been communicated.

So perhaps we could begin to think of writing as a means of communication that provides us, too, with a historical record. While speech is ephemeral, writing is not. Writing enables us to preserve our thoughts over time and to know what individuals removed from us by space and time have thought and communicated. And perhaps, most importantly, writing enables us to participate in the societies and cultures that surround us. It provides us with a highly effective means of communicating our ideas to others.

Kenneth Bruffee, a noted literary critic and scholar, has described this realization of our ability to use language and writing to interact with the social system around us as entering into "the conversation of mankind." Historian Clifford Geertz, in *The Interpretation of Cultures*, has described the phenomenon in this fashion: "Human thought is consummately social: social in its origin, social in its function, social in its forms, social in its applications." *Writing represents one of the most important social applications of human thought.*

"All right, I agree with this idea," you might be saying, "but that still doesn't tell me how to write or how I can learn to write." And you're right, so the question becomes, "How do you learn to write?"

One of the ways your textbook suggests is to become very aware of your own writing process, the myths and rituals you go through before you begin to write. Becoming conscious of the patterns and habits involved for you in the writing act enables you to question whether some of the ideas you believe are helping you or hindering you. Some of the myths you believe about writing might be destructive to your confidence and your motivation; some of the myths might be so erroneous that they lead you down the wrong paths and eventually leave you frustrated and confused, convinced that you will never write well no matter what you do.

So, step number one. Examine the myths that surround your views of writing and see how many of these myths work against you by making you feel too intimidated to write. Step number two, begin the process, suggested by your textbook, of taking a look at the rituals that surround your experience of writing.

Rituals often remain part of an individual's or a culture's experience because of the power they impart. Part of the power of a ritual can be attributed to its regular practice. People perform rituals at particular times in particular ways to achieve particular objectives. As your textbook suggests, establishing a writing ritual for yourself enables you to develop a cluster of behaviors known as a *habit*. A habit is a repeated behavior. Some of our habits, like biting our nails or procrastinating, can be bad for us. Many habits, though, can be highly constructive in enabling us to develop self-discipline and positive motivations. In terms of writing, a good place to begin is to investigate the habits that shape your experience of writing.

For example, do you tend to procrastinate? Do you put things off until the last moment and then have to do a "rush" job to be sure you get your work done? Or are you more disciplined and structured in your work habits, working steadily and persistently on an assignment until it is completed? Are you easily distracted when you start to write? In fact, do you look for distractions (music, TV, the phone ringing, friends visiting, etc.) to keep you from having to get your work done?

Exercise #3

To get a sense of the habits, both good and bad, productive and counterproductive, that surround your writing process, give a brief description of the internal struggles, if any, you go through to write, the attitudes you have developed, the ways you deal with or avoid the work at hand to be done.

One of the joys of being human is that human beings are capable of learning a wide range of behaviors. Human beings are capable of a great deal of change and self-growth. And that is where rituals come in. You will notice that your textbook encourages you to develop a ritual for your writing by suggesting that you find a place, a time, and the tools that make you comfortable and confident enough to write. In fact, your text states, "Every time you use your writing ritual will make the next time you write just that much easier."

Exercise #4

Do you agree with the statement, "Every time you use your writing ritual will make the next time you write just that much easier?" What might there be about rituals that might make it easier for you to write the next time, and the next?

Exercise #5

Describe what, for you, would represent the ideal writing ritual? Are there ways in which your ideal writing ritual conflicts with your present writing ritual? If so, why do you think that might be? What solutions do you propose for resolving that conflict?

One writing ritual, highly recommended for those times when you feel "stuck" on a topic is that of talking yourself through an assignment and becoming aware of your thinking process. Mark Twain, author of *The Adventures of Huckleberry Finn* and many other American literary classics, tells this story about how verbalizing his ideas helped him shape his writing processes:

In the course of twelve years I made six attempts to tell a simple little story which I knew would tell itself in four hours if I could ever find the right starting point. I scored six failures; then one day in London I offered the text of the story to Robert McClure and proposed that he publish that text in the magazine and offer a prize to the person who should tell it best. I became greatly interested and went on talking upon the text for half an hour, then he said: "You have told the story yourself. You have nothing to do but put it on paper just as you have told it."
I recognized that this was true. At the end of four hours it was finished, and

quite to my satisfaction. So it took twelve years and four hours to produce that little bit of a story, which I have called "The Death Wafer."

--The Autobiography of Mark Twain,
ed. Charles Neider.

Never forget the value of expressing your ideas out loud. You'll be amazed at how such a seemingly simple idea can free up your thought processes and enliven your creativity. Some writers even find it highly profitable to speak into a tape recorder as their ideas come to them and then store the ideas for future use and editing. Shifting from the interior world of thought to the external world of speech can often have a very beneficial effect in allowing your ideas to take on the flow and direction they need for clear expression. At the very least, talking out your ideas will give a sense of structure to your pre-writing activities and remove the sense of "floundering around" that so many students experience as they try to write.

Talking out your ideas can help you become more conscious of the inner thought processes that go on during your writing. As your textbook indicates, more people are aware of their external writing rituals--like going to the library at night to write, or making a pot of coffee before undertaking a writing assignment, or sharpening all your pencils before you can begin--than they are of their own inner mental actions. Sometimes this can be the source of many problems with writing. You may spend hours searching for the right opening for your paper, may have drunk the obligatory pot of coffee and sharpened all the pencils in the house, but be totally oblivious to the fact that the strategies you have chosen for undertaking your paper (in essence, for solving the problem writing the assignment presents you with) are not very effective. However, becoming aware of your own composing processes and the strategies you use to design and shape your writing can give you tremendous control over your writing and the power of conscious choice--the power to guide your creative processes and to alter your problem solving techniques as the assignment and its requirements dictate. After all, the ability to develop alternate strategies for reaching goals offers great hope for your improvement and development as a writer.

A great deal of this ability to become aware of your own mental processes and creative strategies can begin with talking out your ideas. Talking out your ideas can really be viewed as a variant of brainstorming, a term originally used in business to describe a "conference method" for solving problems. A group of people gather together and simply start talking about the problem to be solved and reacting to each other's ideas. Ideas are discussed as they "pop up" and no idea is considered too far out or off base to be considered. The result of a brainstorming session is that people have "bounced" ideas off one another, and each idea, in turn, has generated new ideas and new perspectives of thought.

The object of brainstorming is to come up with a list of as many ideas as possible so that you can use the best ideas in your writing. One way to brainstorm

13

might proceed like this. Write your topic down on the top of a blank sheet of paper and list your ideas. Your notes can be single words, phrases, or complete sentences. The form doesn't matter, but writing down quickly as many of your ideas as you can does.

Brainstorming is particularly valuable for the writer because it offers a technique for creative thinking that leads to getting suggestions and approaches for a subject. You can brainstorm with roommates or friends, or you can brainstorm alone by using sheets of scratch paper and recording your ideas as they arise. The important thing is to write down each idea as it comes. Do not censor your thinking process as you brainstorm. Instead, let each idea come as it comes and write it down for further use and speculation. In essence, what you are creating is an association game in which one idea triggers associations for other ideas.

In a certain way, brainstorming is similar to the composing process because brainstorming begins in a random, seemingly disconnected fashion and then becomes more focused or controlled as a topic and an approach to a topic begin to develop. The process allows you to find and shape your subjects, an important and invaluable experience for your writing. Since finding what to write about is a problem for many students, brainstorming offers a good way to begin.

Equally important is finding a way to end a brainstorming session, and one good way is to develop a sense of closure or completeness after each brainstorming session by writing down in a sentence a summary of the most important idea that you have come to. Part of the value of this sentence is that it enables you easily to pick up where you left off, just in case if you return for another brainstorming session or if you decide to use your brainstorming session as a guide or outline, a starting point, for writing your paper.

Brainstorming is very similar to free writing in that you are capturing and writing down ideas as they come, but, in a free writing, you are moving from the random phrases and jotted down ideas of a brainstorming session to develop a kind of "running prose"--parts of sentences and sentences that work in what is often called a "stream of consciousness" fashion. "Stream of consciousness" is a good term for describing this process because your words and ideas do come out in a "stream" of thoughts and associations, and writing down as much of that "stream" as possible will indicate to you just how rich with ideas and how creative your mind can be. In our age of technology for writing and composing, you might find a computer an excellent aid for your free writing exercises in that, if you type or input well, you can capture at greater speed the flow of your ideas than if you are trying to do so writing them out in longhand. As with brainstorming, if you do not stifle or interfere with, censor or judge, inhibit or limit your ideas, you will be amazed and pleased with your ability to write about topics and to come up with insightful things to say.

Free writing loosens you up psychologically and gets the "engine" of your mind and creativity going. The point is to start writing and keep going, without a stop, until you have written down everything you have to say about a particular topic. Only *after* you have done your free writing should you go back and edit what you have written for greater clarity and focus. In a free writing, *never* edit as you write. You will destroy the whole purpose of the exercise.

Remember that free writing means just what it says. Fix your mind on a subject and write nonstop for a period of time. Write freely--that is, do not worry about grammar, punctuation, spelling, etc.--and do not go back and change what you have written. If your mind wanders or your focus shifts, do not interrupt the flow of your ideas or fight the new direction that is developing. You might discover some of your best ideas by letting your mind and your creative processes shape the flow of your ideas, even if, at the time, the direction your ideas move in might seem odd or unimportant to you. A good piece of advice is *follow the flow*! Creativity is a lot less linear and sequential than many people think.

The beauty of free writing, too, is that *just by writing* you allow your mind to shape a perspective upon your subject. Your mind will make connections and generate ideas that you never even thought of, and that is the secret and the secret power of free writing--there is more going on in your mind and your thinking processes than you are consciously aware of at any given minute. Even writers who are convinced that they have nothing to say and will never have anything to say about a particular topic are amazed to discover the range of ideas that flow from their minds if they will just trust the creative processes involved in writing freely.

The most important aspect of free writing is that it enables you to get over your fear that you have nothing to say. You have begun writing, and you can look at the pages you have written freely and see your mind at work. In addition, free writing allows for other opportunities for free writing in that, once you have completed a free writing, you can isolate particular ideas from the first free writing as use them as starting points for other free writings. In this way, you cover a wide range of ideas for your writing assignments.

Here is a sample free writing on the topic of "Dieting" that might indicate to you how this process might work.

No more chocolate cake. 6:00 a.m. walks or jogs. Cottage cheese and melba toast. Oh my god! I can't do this. All my life I've been over weight. Why do I have to change now? Sorority rush coming. Dates and evening dresses. I'll look like a blimp. That's even if I get asked at all. I wish I didn't like food so much. Mom's casseroles are what did this to me. If she wasn't such a good cook, I wouldn't have eaten so much. Wrong. There's always McDonald's. And Pizza Hut. Not to mention the refrigerator. Why am I always so eager to blame someone else for my problem? Maybe I could learn to love green beans. A green bean milk shake. Yuck! A green bean pizza. Getting worse. Maybe a little discipline with what I do eat. Like maybe one sandwich instead of two. Like maybe skipping that afternoon candy bar and Coke. Like maybe eating for my health rather than for my entertainment and pleasure. Like maybe thinking of dieting as a good thing and not as a punishment. Like maybe knowing if I dieted right once and stuck to it I might never have to diet again. Ever.

Now consider what this student did by isolating a topic from her first free writing and generating free writing #2.

Why do I always blame someone else for my weight problem? Like Mom? Like my bone structure? Like genetics, like fate, like God? Because it's easier. And less painful. When I step into the dressing room and I've gone up still another size, I don't have to look in the mirror and say, "Why can't you love yourself enough to have some self-control? Why do you use food for your source of fun and comfort instead of friends and activities? Why do you feel such a need to punish yourself and to fail? Why? Why? Why?" No, instead, I can say, "It's not your fault you're an obese pig. It's your bone structure. You've got big bones, a big frame. You'll never be skinny or petite. Don't blame yourself. Go have a milk shake and cheer yourself up." Who am I kidding? Nobody but me. But it helps. I saw this old movie once on TV, "Lost Weekend," about this alcoholic. His moment of truth comes when he's sitting in a bar and he has to take a look at that it's his hand that's lifting the drink to his mouth, that he's the one controlling both his hand and his mouth. I know the same things, but I'm not always ready to stop eating. Maybe I haven't taken a good enough look at myself. Maybe in a dressing room I'll take a true, good look someday and then I'll know, like the alcoholic knew, I have only myself to blame. Thanks, Mom, for trying to be a scapegoat and for giving me bone structures and genes to blame, but I know it's me. Honest.

This student's first free writing enabled her to develop an idea for her second free writing, which turned out to be a very powerful and and self-revealing piece of writing. Had she continued on, she might have found another topic for a third free writing in her second free writing, and so on. The beauty of free writing is that it easy to do and each free writing opens up a wealth of ideas for further writings.

Free Writing #2

In a free writing, write down your views and feelings about free writing. Do you view free writing as a valuable tool for opening up the creative process? Why might that be? In what ways might you be able to use free writing in your own writing habits and rituals to stimulate creativity?

One of the rituals that your textbook suggests as a way of structuring your writing experience in a more productive and supportive fashion is the keeping of a journal. Many authors attest to how invaluable journals are to them because a journal becomes a history of one's thoughts, a record of the self as it contemplates its existence in the world. Consider, for example, what essayist Joan Didion had to say about journal keeping in *Woman as Writer*.

How it felt to me: that is getting closer to the truth about a notebook. I sometimes delude myself about why I keep a notebook, imagine that some thrifty virtue derives from preserving everything observed. See enough and write it down, I tell myself, and then some morning when the world seems drained of wonder, some day when I am only going through the motions of doing what I am supposed to do, which is write--on that bankrupt morning I will simply open up my notebook and there it will be: a forgotten account with accumulated interest, and passage back to the world out there . . . . I imagine, in other words, that the notebook is about other people. But of course it is not . . . . *Remember what it was to be me*: that is always the point.

Obviously, for many writers, such a recording of impressions and thoughts would be invaluable as a source book of ideas for future writings. Other writers view a journal as an opportunity to engage in a dialogue with their inner selves, to get to know what motivates them and sustains their interest in life, and to have an opportunity to assess, honestly and without fear of judgment from others, their own talents and abilities.

Exercise #6

What do you think of the idea of keeping a journal? Would a journal have much relevance to you? If you were to keep a journal, what types of ideas or thoughts do you think you might record? Do you think you would learn anything new about yourself if you were to keep a journal? What might that be? Do you agree with the view that a journal enables a person to listen to one's inner voice and become familiar with one's deepest concerns? Why do you think that might be? Do you feel any connections exist between that inner voice and the writing process?

Group Exercise #2

As you can tell from the title, this exercise is for the class to perform together. Select one person to go to the blackboard and serve as the recorder for the class. S/he will write the word *Writing* on the board and initiate the process of creating a "Word

Tree." Individuals in the class will call out any words, phrases, or ideas that come to mind in response to this concept. The person at the board will write down each response until a list of terms is developed. Class members will then discuss the terms presented and consider how these terms shed some light on the writing process itself. In other words, what do these terms indicate about how the writing process has been for the class, and how might one develop a sense of the writing process based upon the descriptive adjectives and phrases presented?

Perform the exercise again for the term *Journal Writing*.

What differences in responses are created? How is journal writing viewed by the class? How are these responses similar to or different from the responses given to *Writing*? Which of the terms, *Writing* or *Journal Writing*, was received more favorably? Why does the class think that might be?

Often journal writing is met with a great deal less enthusiasm than the idea of writing in general, largely because people can often see more use for writing in their daily lives than for journal writing, and because journal writing, as it is often described, seems to them to require a higher degree of discipline than other types of writing. Often they respond with the idea that if they tried to write in a journal every day they would have nothing to say. They believe their ideas are not that interesting and that they would not have enough original ideas to record.

Two misperceptions need to be corrected here, and one is that a person has to write in a journal every day. Certainly, this structure would be the ideal arrangement because it would generate a degree of discipline and attentiveness in the person learning to write, but the world is full of very accomplished writers who write in their journals as events or interests dictate. The second misperception is that a journal is only for the recording of unique and original ideas.

Actually, in truth, few of us will be using our journals to write profound philosophical insights, the likes of which the world has never seen or heard before. Most of us will be recording our thoughts, perceptions, and feelings in our journals, and that is exactly as it should be, for a journal is, above all else, a record book. We use our journals to record our ideas, and the end result of that process is that we get in touch with our thinking processes and with our writing voice by being attentive to and responsive to what our ideas are trying to tell us.

Sounds simple and easy, doesn't it? The truth is, though, that the idea of keeping a journal creates in most people a deep sense of fear and resistance. Simply put, we balk at the idea because journal keeping involves a measure of risk and of self-disclosure. "What if I try recording my thoughts and find out I have nothing to say?" students often suggest. Or, "What if I record my thoughts and find out how boring I am?"

Sometimes the excuses are less metaphysical and more pragmatic. "I don't have the time." "What if someone finds my journal and reads it?" "I could spend the time involved in keeping a journal to do something more useful." "I don't see the value of keeping a journal; why do I have to do it?"

Interestingly, the pragmatic concerns are often answered by resolving the metaphysical issues. In essence, people seem to find the time to do what they really want to do, or what they seem to think has value and meaning for them. Many an exhausted college student who couldn't lift another finger, couldn't open a single book to study, seems magically to find boundless energy when asked to a party or given free tickets to a concert. We all tend to view the world from our own value schema, and what we value we pursue and attend to.

If this axiom is true, how can the value of journal writing be discovered? Perhaps the simplest way is to keep a journal for a period of time and see what value it has for you. While you are a student in a composition class, a journal might prove invaluable in helping you to get in touch with your writing voice, the flow of ideas going on in your mind as you think. After all, these ideas are the source of all that you will write about, since every one of your essays will begin in the flow of your ideas about a particular topic.

In addition, keeping a journal helps strengthen the skills of observation and self-awareness, both important abilities to have in the writing process. Many assignments you will produce for your composition class, as well as for the professional world you will enter, will depend upon your ability to observe and record in detail. Other types of writing assignments will call upon your capacity for self-awareness, or your skill at understanding your responses and assessing your viewpoints and feelings.

In many ways, keeping a journal is similar to the free writing exercises emphasized by your textbook. In a journal, as in a free writing, you write out your ideas in a flow, as they come to you, unedited and uncritiqued. The focus is upon the flow of ideas and not, at that particular moment, upon correctness of style or measuring up to all the "rules" about writing that you think might exist. To get in touch with your ideas and to see how easily they flow and develop if you do not inhibit, censor, harshly judge, or set up unreasonable expectations for your writing, are the purposes of journal writing, just as they are in a free writing.

Exercise #7

Use a free writing that you have done in class as the basis for a journal entry. What differences and similarities do you find in these two types of writing? Which do you feel is more valuable for you, in the long run, as a developing writer? Do you feel there really is such a thing as a "free writing," or are we always, as writers, aware of rules and restrictions upon our writing styles and content? Do you feel a journal entry is more or less "free" than a free writing?"

Point/Counterpoint: Considering Opposing Arguments

The purpose of this section is to introduce you to an important concept in critical thinking, the refutation. The idea of the refutation is that truth often is not simple and clear-cut and that arguments, statements, and premises can be seen from a number of angles.

A refutation considers the opposing argument(s) to propositions or points of view that have been developed. Learning to think of opposing arguments and to evaluate the merit of both the original argument (the point being made) and its opposite (the counterpoint) are important dimensions of critical thinking.

In each of the questions/exercises that follow, you are asked to write an essay in which you evaluate premises or ideas that have been presented to you by your textbook or your workbook. Your task/assignment is to assess the merit of these ideas, the validity of their claims. Essentially, if the case made for the original argument, position A, seems interesting and convincing, how will considering position B (A's opposite) affect your view of A?

Point/Counterpoint, or antiphonal thinking, will help you look at ideas from a number of perspectives. This capacity to see the complexity involved with ideas and the claims they make to truth and accuracy will help add depth and greater insight to your critical thinking skills.

1. In Chapter One, several students discuss their writing rituals and practices, and one of the students makes the statement, "Once I get past my writer's block, I see that I can be a good writer."

What do you think the student means by the word *see* here? What does it mean for him to *see* that he can be a good writer, as opposed to *believe*, *hope*, or *know*? Would the idea here change if he had stated, "Once I get past my writer's block, I *know* I can be a good writer."

How about yourself? Do you *see* you can be a better writer, or *hope* that you can? Do you *believe* that you can be a better writer, or *know* that you can?

What do you think happens to people when they *see* that they can do something? What do you think it takes for a person to *see* in this way? Do you relate this way of *seeing* to motivation? In what way?

2. Another student in Chapter One describes what for him seems to be a fairly successful "writing ritual"--gathering up all his materials, getting on his bike, riding to campus, and setting himself up in the art lounge in the student center. No distractions. Quiet. The camaraderie of other people hard at work. A different setting and surroundings.

What do you think of this "writing ritual"? Do you think the ritual itself--the leaving home and going to the student center in the evenings--has as much to do with the writing itself, or is it the dedicated commitment to getting his work done that makes the student so successful in accomplishing his aims? Do you agree with the idea that to get your writing done you would have to agree to give your writing some measure of time and focused attention? Why might that be?

3. In Chapter One, "Myths and Rituals," Stephen Reid, the author of your textbook, gives you one model of how the writing process works and of how writers go about that process: writing rituals, keeping journals, lots of warm-up exercises like free writing to get you started.

Do you agree with this model? Is this the way you go about your writing?

Does this model seem, to you, more appropriate to people who are "stuck" and don't know how to begin, than to people with a strong sense of conviction about what they want to write about? Suppose someone really angered you and you had to write back a response? Would you go through the process Reid describes in writing your response? Would you need a writing ritual--a certain place to go to at a certain time? Would you need to keep a journal in order to express your anger? Would you need a lot of free writing exercises? Similarly, suppose you wanted to tell somebody how thrilled you were about receiving first prize in a contest? Would Reid's model of the writing process still apply?

4. Do you think Reid's model might best describe the process *students* have to go through to write English papers on topics assigned to them that they don't have a lot of interest in? You know the type, "Why Have You Chosen to Come to College?" "Why Did You Pick This College?" "What Are Your Plans for Your Future?" "Should Abortion Be Legalized?" "What Is the Best Advice You've Ever Been Given?" Is it possible that the model Reid gives best describes how one must go about writing papers on topics one has little enthusiasm for? Or is it possible that following the model your textbook describes will generate enthusiasm for a particular topic? What do you think?

5. In describing his model of the writing process, Reid uses quotations from a number of writers, including Gore Vidal, Doris Lessing, Ernest Hemingway, Edna O'Brien, Gabriel Garcia Marquez, Gloria Steinem, Margaret Atwood, Maria Irene Fornes, Ntzoake Shange, Donald Murray, Toni Cade Bambara, and E. M. Forster, to support his position. Most of these authors, ten out of twelve, are creative writers-- novelists, short story writers, or playwrights; the remaining two, Gloria Steinem and Donald Murray, are essayists.

Keeping a journal seems to be of value to creative writers, but do you think keeping a journal is more appropriate to creative writers, who often depend upon memory and accurate descriptions of a range of details for their writing, than it is to other types of writers?

Do you feel that keeping a journal would work for other types of writing, or other types of settings? Like business or technical writing, for example? Would you find much value in keeping a journal if you were working and writing in a business or professional setting? If you wouldn't find a journal of much help in this setting, could you imagine any type of writing exercises or practices that you would find of value and would recommend?

6. In *Zen and the Art of Motorcycle Maintenance*, a book about theories of knowledge, Robert M. Pirsig devotes a section to describing his experience of teaching freshman English for several years in Montana. [Note that *he* and *Phaedrus* in this section refer to Pirsig himself]:

What you're supposed to do in most freshman rhetoric courses is to read a little essay or short story, discuss how the writer has done certain little things to achieve certain little effects, and then have the students write an imitative little essay or short story to see if they can do the same little things. He tried this over and over again but it never jelled. The students seldom achieved anything, as a result of this calculated mimicry, that was remotely close to the models he'd given them. More often their writing got worse. It seemed as though every rule he honestly tried to discover with them was so full of exceptions and contradictions and qualifications and confusions that he wished he'd never come across the rule in the first place.
A student would always ask how the rule would apply in a certain special circumstance. Phaedrus would then have the choice of trying to fake through a made-up explanation of how it worked, or follow the selfless route and say what he really thought. And what he really thought was that the rule was *pasted on* to the writing after the writing was all done. It was *post hoc*, after the fact, instead of prior to the fact. And he became convinced that all the writers the students were supposed to mimic wrote without rules, putting down whatever sounded right, then going back to see if it still sounded right and changing it if it didn't. There were some who apparently wrote with calculating premeditation because that's the way their product looked. But that seemed to him to be a very poor way to look. It had a certain syrup, as Gertrude Stein once said, but it didn't pour. But how're you to teach something that isn't premeditated? It was a seemingly impossible requirement.

What do you think of Pirsig's assessment? Do you agree with his idea that the rules of writing do not evolve from the act of writing itself, but are *pasted on, after the fact,* by those who wish to systematize writing and break it down into parts, rules, sections, and pieces for the sake of studying writing and trying to figure out how it is done? Do you agree with his view that it is "a seemingly impossible requirement" to "teach something that isn't premeditated?"
What about his view of how writing is taught? Do you agree that students are presented with writings from famous authors and encouraged to imitate the styles and organizational patterns they find there? Do you think this is an effective way to teach writing? Do you feel that imitation leads to true learning and understanding, or only to more imitation? Were you taught to write in this way, or by other means?
Do you feel that the writers the students are studying became excellent writers

by imitating others, or by trusting their inner creative processes and instincts for what is good in writing--or, as Pirsig describes it, "putting down whatever sounded right, then going back to see if it still sounded right and changing it if didn't?" If Pirsig is right and the writing process is unpremeditatedly creative and therefore truly cannot be taught because each writing process will be unique to the individual, what value do you find in studying the writing process broken down and segmented into parts after the fact?

7. Stephen Reid, the author of your textbook, says the important thing to remember as you go about learning to write is that you "are already a writer."

Do you agree with this statement? If you "already are a writer," do you need this workbook, your textbook, or even this writing class? What value will any of these serve you if you "already are a writer?"

SUMMARY AND ASSESSMENT PAGE

What ideas from *CHAPTER ONE: MYTHS AND RITUALS* (in either your textbook or your workbook) helped you the most with your writing? What ideas or techniques did you hope to get from this chapter but did not? What steps do you intend to take to learn those ideas or techniques?

*"**THE DESIRE TO WRITE GROWS WITH WRITING**"*

--ERASMUS

CHAPTER TWO: PURPOSE AND PROCESS FOR WRITING

Many students think of writing as a procedure, with a straightforward, unvarying set of steps to follow, rather than as a process. Viewing writing as a procedure, they want simple guidelines or blueprints they can follow with little deviation from a standard and certainly without any great concern for creativity and individual variations.

If writing were a procedure, like let's say changing a flat tire or putting together a model airplane, it would be easy to specify the steps one would follow. First you do this, then you do that; follow steps one, two, three, four, five, six, seven, eight, nine, and then, voila, the well-made essay! Wouldn't that be grand?

Indeed, it would, but writing is not a procedure. In fact, the belief that writing is a procedure (or can be learned in the way one masters a procedure) is one of the most limiting and pervasive views about writing. It is one of the "myths" about writing that many students believe. No wonder that when they try to learn writing as if it were a procedure with quick and easy steps to follow, they become frustrated and confused and many times give up on the whole affair entirely.

The view that writing is a procedure is a very comforting one, and one that many students are reluctant to give up--even though often this view proves erroneous and limiting. The belief that writing can be procedurized make it all seem simpler somehow, and manageable. Learn the procedure and write like a professional.

Sounds almost like a magazine ad, doesn't it? "For $19.95, you, too, can get the *Writing Procedure Manual* and write like a pro! Hurry now and place your order. If you call before 5:00 p.m., we'll throw in a set of steak knives and a bamboo steamer absolutely free!"

Sounds too good to be true, doesn't it? And that's because it is. Only in a very few instances does writing follow a procedural form, and often these are examples of business and technical writing (such as memos, certain types of business letters and reports, and instructional manuals) in which the focus is upon transactional writing, or writing designed to ensure that a certain job gets done. This type of writing, the core of which involves giving directions or instructions, or making a request, lends itself rather easily to a formulaic or procedural organizational pattern. Most other types of writing, though, do not.

Often students are introduced to writing through "beginner's practice exercises" that make the process of writing well seem more formulaic and less complex than it is. These practice exercises give one a place to begin, much like a music student learns the scales as the initial stage of his or her instruction. The assumption is never that the student will learn to play the scales and *only* the scales, or that the scales should be learned as an end in themselves. Learning the scales represents a first step toward mastery, a stage along the way, and not the way itself.

In writing, the equivalent to learning the scales is often instruction in the three-point enumeration essay, also sometimes called "the five-paragraph essay. This is one pattern for writing an essay, and it is essentially a beginner's learning exercise. What it calls for is taking a topic, any topic, and breaking it down into: (1) an introductory paragraph in which the thesis is stated and sub-divided into three supporting ideas; (2) three paragraphs of development, each of which is devoted to a discussion of one of the three points enumerated in the introductory paragraph; and (3) a summary concluding paragraph in which the thesis and the three supporting ideas are restated (summarized). Here is an example of a three-point enumeration essay written in response to the topic, "Discuss the Causes of the Civil War."

The Civil War of 1861-65 was caused by the inequities of the slavery system, the Westward expansion, and economic difficulties. These three factors accounted for one of the most destructive wars in American history.

The slavery system that existed in America until nearly the end of the nineteenth century created great conflicts in the American social and political systems between the ethics of the correct treatment of human beings and the practical issues of the slave economy. In part, the War was caused by the inability of either side to find a solution in which both ethics and economics could be reconciled.

The Westward expansion aggravated the problem because many abolitionists did not want slavery to expand out of the South and into the West, while many pro-slavery advocates saw slavery as essential to fostering a new and undeveloped region. Since this was again basically a conflict between morality and money, a compromise was not reached.

The economic difficulties that beset the North and the South in the first half of the nineteenth century also contributed to making matters worse. Both the North and the South were struggling for markets in Europe, and both relied upon different means to attract those markets. The South put its faith in agriculture, which required a labor-intensive economy, but not one that could sustain high labor costs since the profit margin in agriculture was both narrow and more unpredictable. The North put its faith in manufacturing, which could allow for higher labor costs because of a more predictable manufacturing cycle of supply and demand. Manufacturing also allowed for mechanization at a higher pace than did agriculture, and thus the labor force issue could be secondary in the North while it was primary in the South.

As a result of the slavery system, the Westward expansion, and economic difficulties, the Civil War took its costly toll on America and remained one of America's most controversial and destructive wars. Perhaps the struggle might have been avoided if both sides had been willing to negotiate compromises between difficult issues of ethics and economics.

While this essay has an effective and clear style and a good focus on content, its organizational pattern is very simple and also very easy to identify. In fact, the organizational pattern detracts from the essay because it makes the essay predictable and therefore less engrossing and engaging.

Perhaps more important to our discussion is the fact that this topic lends itself to division into three parts more readily than a number of other topics for which such a division would be difficult indeed. In fact, why not try imitating this three-part structure for an exercise on the following topic.

Exercise #1

Write a three-point enumeration essay on the following topic: "My most important memories."

How did it go? Odds are that you couldn't so easily fit your important memories into such a formulaic structure, or, if you could, that your essay came out sounding very stilted and slightly insincere. After all, who really wants to read or believes an essay that starts off: "My most important memories are the birth of my brother, my graduation from high school, and the day my mother received her college degree."

This type of writing is not very engaging and violates a major concept of good writing presented to you by your textbook: "Most good writing has a personal dimension. It may be about the writer personally or it may address a subject or an idea the writer cares about. It begins in honesty, curiosity, inquiry, and vulnerability. Good writers assert themselves, knowing that they are vulnerable to other people's criticism . . . . By continually probing and learning, being honest with themselves, and accepting the risks, writers can use their writing to teach themselves and others."

Many writers feel, however, that if they are writing about themselves and about events from their lives that they *are* expressing a "personal dimension" in their writing. This is an inaccurate perception, though, because there is more to having a "personal dimension" to one's writing than simply writing about one's own feelings.

The concept of a "personal dimension" or "voice" in writing is highly valued by most readers. Writing that is representative of a unique and interesting way of looking at things and that is expressed in an engaging style is highly preferable to writing that takes a trite approach presented in a predictable and stilted fashion.

Exercise #2

How would you define "voice" or the "personal dimension" in writing? How do you recognize "voice" in writing? What are its characteristics? Why do you think "voice" is so important to good writing? Do you feel you are good at expressing your "voice" in writing, or do you feel this is an area that is difficult for you and will require a degree of work?

Exercise #3

Return to your textbook and reconsider the essay, "Writing for Myself," by Russell Baker. How would you define the "voice" in this essay? Do you think this essay possesses a "personal dimension" to its style and structure? What is the relationship Baker assumes between his essay and himself, and between himself and his audience?

Group Exercise #1

Divide the class into groups of four or five students, and have each group work on recasting Russell Baker's essay into a three-point enumeration essay. Have a designated member of each group read the essays out loud, and let the class engage in critiquing each essay for the qualities that make for good writing. At the end of the exercise, have the class work toward a "To Do" and "Not to Do" list on how to write if one hopes to generate interesting and intrinsically coherent prose that captures and engages a reader's attention.

"Voice," or the "personal dimension" in writing, is essentially the projection of the writer's personality onto the written page. It is the way the writer chooses to be encountered by the reader and the degree of self-disclosure the writer is willing to reveal.

Interestingly enough, natural expression does not necessarily come naturally. Often it takes time and thought, usually in the rewriting process. In producing your draft, think of your writing from the point of view of someone who knows you well and replace any language that person would say was "not you." A good rule of thumb is *don't write it if you wouldn't say it*. If you want your papers to sound like you, then write them the way you would say them. That is the essence of personal voice and the easiest way to avoid stuffiness and artificiality in your writing. Ask yourself, "Would I really say this this way?" If the answer is no, edit and revise your prose for a more natural style. For example, consider this opening from a student paper: "It was on the day after my high school graduation that I commenced the process of considering the myriad roads and opportunities that lay before me as I reflected upon what direction I should choose for my future."

Honestly, do you think that anyone would ever talk like this to someone else? Could you imagine this type of prose occurring naturally in a conversation? In all probability, the student would be more likely to say something like: "The day after graduation I started thinking about all the opportunities that lay ahead and what I should do with my future." This prose sounds much more like a person talking to another and passes the "cup of coffee test." In seeking a personal voice for your prose, write as you would sound in talking to a friend over a cup of coffee. If your prose doesn't sound like you would sound in this setting, cut, edit, and revise until you sound like you expressing yourself in your own way and in your own words.

Free Writing #1

Discuss your writing in terms of your own "personal voice." Does writing in a "personal voice" come easily to you, or it is difficult for you to do? Have you been encouraged by others, especially your teachers, to write in a "personal voice," or have you been encouraged to be more formal and objective with your writing?

An interesting fact of the writing process is that we do not always project the same voice in all our writings. The letter you write to your friend, Joe, about your job search will be quite different from the letter you write to your academic advisor. Our thoughts and our experiences are composed of many voices, and we creatively select the voice, persona, or aspect of self we wish to share with our audience. This complexity adds a great deal of magic and mystery to the writing process and indicates how intricate the process truly is.

Many writers feel strongly that it is not necessary to reveal a great deal of the self in writing, that their purpose is only to convey information and respond to the assignment. Actually, though, this is an impossibility, for every language choice a writer makes is in some way indicative of the way that his or her mind works. Although the degree may vary from composition to composition, writing is always self-disclosing. This, too, is part of the process and part of the mystery of writing well. And it is extremely important to emphasize that writing *is* a process that requires patience, practice, and an acceptance of one's limitations. Very few writers in very, very few instances will write a perfect essay on the first draft. Nearly all writers will grapple with the process of writing until they improve their work and move toward mastery of written expression.

Free Writing #2

What has the process of writing been like for you? Has learning to write come easily and quickly to you, or has it been a struggle?

The alternative to viewing writing as a procedure is to view it as a process. A process suggests an ongoing movement, a progression, while a procedure suggests a pre-determined set of steps to follow. Another way to phrase this contrast is to say that a procedure is static and relatively unchanging, while a process is organic and often in flux, or a state of change. Procedures, too, are largely impersonal. They are structured in such a way that anybody who follows this set of steps or directions will come out with the anticipated same result. By and large, very few unique personal twists are placed upon procedures, while a process often not only invites but almost necessitates a high degree of personal investment. The creative energy and uniqueness of the individual are what make a process flow, while, with a procedure, it is steps followed in a sequence that ensure a specified and pre-determined outcome.

Here is another important difference, too. In a procedure, the outcome is known, or at least predictable. In a process, the outcome is only guessed at, and the final outcome may be entirely different from the original idea of the outcome with which one started.

Consider again the example, in your textbook, of Russell Baker's essay, "Writing for Myself." His original objective was to write an essay on "The Art of Eating Spaghetti" to fulfill a writing assignment in Mr. Fleagle's third-year English class. Instead, look what happened. As Baker says, when he read this topic on the homework sheet, the title "produced an extraordinary sequence of mental images. Surging up out of the depths of memory came a vivid recollection of a night in Belleville . . . ."

And then the essay began to take on a life and a character of its own because a memory had stirred Baker's creative *process*. All of a sudden, in one magical, mysterious, creative moment, he no longer is writing about "The Art of Eating Spaghetti," but about his loving feelings for his family. And in this *process*, he is discovering that he wanted to write for himself, and not Mr. Fleagle. And apparently, from Mr. Fleagle's and the class's response, Baker wrote a powerful and engaging essay that captured the specialness of that night with his family. Even further, this episode in Baker's high school English class set him to thinking about the idea of being a writer, an idea, he admits, that had never before even entered his mind. Most definitely for Baker, this outcome could never have been foreseen as he began his essay on "The Art of Eating Spaghetti."

Had Baker simply been following a procedure in writing his essay, he might have started, "The art of eating spaghetti involves good eye-hand coordination, patience, and a liking for Italian food. Each of these three factors is highly important to the art of eating spaghetti, or the fine art of pasta appreciation." A paragraph of discussion on each of the three points, a summary conclusion, and the essay would have been completed.

Completed, yes, but how well? Would this truly be an engaging essay, one that you would *want* to read and would read with great personal interest and investment? Or would it be, at best, merely informative? Would it possess a personal dimension or "voice," or would it seem the type of essay that anybody anywhere could have written with a minimum of investment and time?

Here might be a helpful way to look at the process/procedure distinction. As a general rule, essays that follow or imitate a formula or procedure are less interesting and draw a lesser degree of reader response than essays that evolve organically from a process. Most readers prefer "voice" (the personal dimension) in writing to writing that seems impersonal and formulaic. Often the "voice" in a particular piece of writing will not evolve until the formal constraints, the procedures to be followed, are removed. Free writings provide this opportunity by removing any sense of constraint upon an individual's writing and by refusing to specify the particular form that that writing is to take in order to be considered "acceptable" or "correct."

Perhaps now it might be clearer why your textbook encourages free writings as a way to begin and stimulate your own creative process. Often it is only in removing the constraints that you find out how good a writer you really are. In other words, how well can you write if you *don't* follow a procedure? Could you even write at all?

The answer is yes, even though you might not think so at the time--especially if you have become heavily dependent upon formulaic writing and have managed to do fairly well with it in terms of grades and meeting deadlines. Perhaps your psychology is, "If X works, why change it?" Simple. X might be impeding your growth as a writer.

When in doubt, try P-R-O-C-E-S-S:

PERCEIVE

the dimensions of the assignment that has been given you. What are you being asked to do in the assignment? This is an essential first step because writing that does not fulfill the terms and requirements of the assignment is seldom valued very highly. No matter how well you may write upon a topic unrelated or only tangentially related to the original assignment, the odds are that misinterpreting or failing to understand the original assignment will count against you. There is, too, a fine line between misinterpreting an assignment (which indicates an error in interpretation) and not being able to do the assignment (which indicates a lack of conceptual strategies), so be sure that you avoid having either of these interpretations placed upon your writing.

RECORD

your ideas about the assignment. Perhaps you will make an extensive outline, or perhaps only jot down a few notes to yourself. Perhaps you will "brainstorm" or do a "free writing," but, whatever method you decide upon, be sure to keep a good record of both your thoughts and your thinking processes. This record, or pre-draft, will prove invaluable to you in the later stages of writing your essay.

ORGANIZE

your thoughts into a strategy of presentation. This strategy will involve such issues as a sense of "voice" and audience, as well as an idea of what types of reasoning and supporting conclusions will persuade your readers of the merit of your point of view.

Organizing your ideas into a pattern that can be interpreted and appreciated by others is a primary concern of writing well. Disorganized writing makes it exceedingly difficult for you to get your ideas across effectively, while organized writing makes your audience aware of the impact of your ideas. All forms of writing, whether imaginative (creative and fictional) or factual and informative, both depend upon and reveal an underlying organizational pattern for the expression of their ideas. Developing an appropriate and effective pattern that will address the requirements of a particular writing assignment will be an important aspect, for you, of the writing process.

CONCEPTUALIZE

the impact of your writing. In other words, envision the result you want your to writing to have for your audience. If you want them to be impressed with the nuances and intricacies of your writing style, you will have to spend time and care crafting your sentence structures and assessing the efficacy of your vocabulary choices. If you want your audience to embrace and take to heart the recommendations you are urging, you will need to choose wisely the means of persuasion you will use. Conceptualizing your writing will allow you the opportunity to envision how your writing will be perceived by others and thus anticipate and structure the types of responses to your writing you wish to achieve.

EVALUATE

the quality of the thought (and thinking processes) your writing will embody. This step will require honesty, sincerity, and self-awareness of your part. It is often tempting and easy for us to overvalue our own writing simply because it is our own work. In this stage of the process, it is important for you to assess, weigh out, and consider the degree of thought you have put into the assignment. Essentially, have you demonstrated a capacity for critical thinking, or the ability to consider an idea fairly from a number of angles, or have you simply responded with the most obvious and apparent response that has required very little thought at all? Simplistic thinking makes for simplistic writing. Evaluate your ideas to be sure that you have dealt with the assignment on a full and complex, rather than a superficial, level.

STRUCTURE

your ideas into a first draft. Write out your ideas in the atmosphere of a "free writing," without the inhibiting constraints of worrying about getting every detail of the paper correct the first time through. Allow yourself the encouragement and the freedom to write down your ideas and to try out your organizational strategies without being critical of yourself as you write. After you have completed the first draft, then you will have any number of opportunities for corrections and revisions. At this point, you need the opportunity to put your ideas together to see how they are working and what might need to be changed.

SYNTHESIZE

your skills and your ideas to take your writing through from its first draft to its final version. Here you will need to become a critic of your own work, and that is often difficult to do well. Many of us are too critical of ourselves and wind up creating a "writer's block," instead, in which we cannot write at all without a voice in our heads saying, "This isn't any good at all. You can't write. You might as well quit trying." Others of us are too lax and are willing to settle for anything so long as it is done and we can turn it in. The important issue here is to obtain a balance between your desire for finishing the assignment and for producing the best work that you can. This balance will necessitate a concern with the design of your writing, as well as a focus upon a fluid and clear style, correct use of grammar and mechanics, and careful proofreading. In this final stage, you are the editor deciding upon the merit of this essay. Praise yourself fully for what you have accomplished in finishing the drafts of your paper, and then get down to some very serious and careful editing for the final draft of your paper to ensure that good organization, a fluent and expressive style, and careful proofreading for correct spelling, grammar, and mechanics will prevail.

Your textbook offers you this same P-R-O-C-E-S-S, but with a different set of terms: collecting, shaping, drafting, and revising. This is an excellent sequence, for no one can write without collecting his or her ideas about a topic, shaping those ideas into some type of rudimentary organizational pattern, drafting a rough version of the written essay, and revising that version until it becomes a well-structured and well-expressed essay.

For many writers, revision is the hardest part of the writing process, for it is very difficult, once they have written an essay, to re-envision or re-see that essay anew in order to revise it. A good place to begin is to ask, "What is the essay's focus?"

In "Murder in a Bottle" by John Lempesis, the essay's theme or topic is a persuasive argument against drunk driving. The essay's focus is to develop that argument through the use of powerful narrative examples that personalize the issue of drunk driving by showing its effects upon people's lives. The focus of the essay allows the essay to be far more moving and persuasive than if Lempesis had chosen to write an article that presented a statistical analysis of drunk driving accidents in America over the last ten years. Awareness of the focus of his article also allows Lempesis the opportunity to see if he has fulfilled his purpose in the essay by checking the design of the essay against its original purpose or focus.

Exercise #4

Consider "Murder in a Bottle" from the angle of its focus. How would the essay be changed if the focus were shifted to a statistical analysis of the impact of drunk driving? In what others ways could you imagine the focus of this essay might be altered? How would each of these changes affect the impact and significance of the essay for its audience?

Exercise #5

In what ways is focus related to purpose in an essay? How does clarifying the focus of an essay clarify its purpose? In what ways are focus and purpose related to issues of audience in writing an essay?

One way to view the focus of an essay is to consider how it is related to the logical plan or organization of your essay as a whole. The focus directs the reader's attention to the points you wish to make in your essay, and the logical plan or organization of the essay (the structure) allows your reader to understand when and why you move from one point to another.

Structure is crucial to a well-written essay, and it is usually very apparent when an essay lacks and effective structure. If the logical plan or organization of an essay is weak, the ideas of the essay seem disconnected or randomly co-joined. Paragraphs within the essay can be moved from place to place with no apparent loss of meaning or power. In fact, paragraphs can often be cut entirely and little is lost. Essays that lack structure often ramble, repeat themselves, or fail to develop ideas beyond stating them in very obvious and superficial ways. Essays with good structure indicate that the writer has carefully thought out and dealt with the implications of his or her ideas and of how to express them effectively to others.

Perhaps an easy way to consider if your essay has good structure is to ask yourself if your points make sense. Are you developing a convincing argument with sound reasoning and support, or are you simply presenting ideas that appeal to you and interest you but that add little of substance to the merit of your ideas?

Group Exercise #2

Here is a good way for the class to check out the hypothesis that a logical plan of organization is essential to the quality of an essay's achievement. In this exercise, the class is divided into groups of four or five, and each group is asked to evaluate the merit of five essays written in response to the topic of whether the writer agrees with or disagrees with French philosopher Jean-Paul Sartre's statement, "We are our choices."

Each of the essays is to be evaluated for the merit or quality of its structure, as well as for the quality and depth of the argument it is making. Essentially, does the essay exhibit a logical plan of organization sufficient to deal with the ideas it is considering, and, secondly, is the argument that is made a convincing one?

Each of the groups is to evaluate the essays in any method it chooses, although the process of awarding grades from "A" through "F" is the more common practice. After the essays have been evaluated, each group will work up a description of what constitutes good structure in an essay and of how structure is to be evaluated and assessed.

Essay #1: "Choices"

I agree with Sartre's statement. I mean, what else could we be but our choices? We choose the kind of food we eat, and I heard on the news the other day that certain kinds of diets can cause diseases like cancer and heart trouble. This would be an example of how our choices could affect who we are. I know from experience that the food you eat can have an effect upon you. I am allergic to wheat, and whenever I eat wheat I break out in a rash. If I made a different choice, I wouldn't get sick.

It's not just food that is part of the choices we make. There are also jobs. If I study to be an engineer, that's a choice I make. There are also marriage and children. You choose these things, and that's why I think Sartre is right about our choices making us who we are.

Money is another area where there's a lot of choice. My uncle Harry lost a lot of money investing in stocks. He bought stock in a meat processing company, and it went bankrupt. Nobody made him do that, and he'd be the first one to say it was his own fault.

So, from the idea that we control the food we eat, the way we dress, the jobs we have, and whether we have marriages and children, I would agree with Sartre's statement that we are our choices.

Essay #2: "Is It Really Up to Us?"

If you could be anything you wanted to--what would you be? Would you be the same, or would you drastically change? Jean-Paul Sartre states, "We are our choices." If this were true, wouldn't we all be millionaires, fashion models, or something more exciting than the position we presently occupy? I have to disagree with Sartre. I feel that there are certain limitations to what we can do and therefore become.

While Sartre would say that a person's life is shaped by the choices he or she makes, I believe a person's life is just as influenced by things over which he has no control. For example, the main limitations that hinder a person in pursuit of his choices are circumstances (or fate, if you will) and an individual's abilities. These two barriers are often extremely hard, if not impossible, to change. Therefore, I feel we tend to make compromises about our choices and settle for the best possible situation. For instance, Joe wants to go to college and land a fantastic job upon graduation. However, Joe's family is financially troubled and unable to put him through college. On the other hand, suppose Joe receives financial aid enabling him to attend. Joe receives failing marks in all classes because his academic skills are weak. In the first situation, Joe's environment is limiting his choices, just as his academic ability, or lack thereof, would have rendered Joe unable to graduate. It turns out that Joe is good with engines and he decides to work in that field. He is able to make some money for the family and is relatively happy. I believe many people fall prey to this type of "compromise and settle" pattern. I wish to pilot airplanes but can't because of my poor eyesight. A handicapped child wants to run, skip rope, or dance, but is unable. Each individual is unique. It is this uniqueness that is the separating factor in the choices that each individual has to make.

I agree with Sartre's basic ideas on the impact of choice. However, I feel that Sartre would argue that the compromise or reevaluation of a choice is a choice in itself. I disagree; rather, I would argue that our lives are made up of a series of compromises stemming from our limited choices. Sartre may also argue that I have misinterpreted his original meaning of choice. He may be speaking of the choices that each individual makes after he discovers his limitations. I extracted from Sartre's quotation, "We are our choices," a rather holistic ideal that we can choose and therefore become anything we desire. Instead of the idea that we are our choices, aren't our choices or types of choices dictated by the limitations upon us?

Essay #3: "Are We Our Choices?"

Sartre's statement, "We are our choices," seems to suggest that our identity is defined by the choices we make, and only by those choices. I have a great deal of difficulty accepting so broad a generalization as this. Certainly, there are many choices we do make that do have an effect upon our identity. We choose our friends, our religious beliefs, the community we live in, our careers, interests, and hobbies. Ultimately, we even choose if we are going to exist at all, for suicide is always an option--a choice--in any moment of human existence. With this aspect of Sartre's argument, I have no quarrel. However, I feel that there are many elements that affect and define human identity that are beyond our control and therefore not of our own choosing.

Many psychologists, Freud included, have argued that much of our identity is established by the time we reach the age of six. The upbringing we receive from our parents and the psychological tensions of any given family unit have a profound effect upon the type of personality we develop. If our early childhood affects us adversely, we can develop neuroses, psychoses, psychosomatic illnesses, subconscious emotional hangups--many mental and emotional problems, in essence, that will affect us for the rest of our lives and determine our personality structure. All of these influential factors from our upbringing would occur before we were adults and thus even had the power, let alone the means and the opportunity, to make

41

personal choices.

I would argue, too, that only a truly naive person could believe that "reality" has no effect upon limiting or influencing our choices. Our genetic makeup is given to us at the moment of conception, and that makeup determines how we will be received in society. If I am born to a certain race or a certain gender that my society discriminates against, I will suffer many personal hurts that will affect my identity, as well as experience a severe limiting of my choices by society. My genetic makeup will determine, too, my resistance to certain types of illnesses. Can I honestly argue that I can choose to be healthy? Certainly, there are many things, such as diet and exercise, I can do to keep myself in good health, but if I inherit a genetic or metabolic disorder that makes me develop juvenile diabetes, this disorder will not be my choice, but it certainly will influence who I am and the kinds of choices I will be able to make in the future.

I assume by Sartre's statement that he is not an economic determinist like Herbert Spencer or Karl Marx. Poverty and wealth have a profound effect upon the kinds of opportunities I will have and therefore the kinds of choices I can make. If I have to struggle working three jobs to get through college, I possibly will make lower grades than someone who has his way paid completely. My lower grades, heavily influenced by my economic circumstances, will determine what kind of professional future I can have. My choices will be affected by the choices I could not make because of economic circumstances. Thus, can I say at this point that who I am is the result of my choices, or should I say that who I am is the result of the choices I did not get to make? I would answer that who I am is a combination of the choices I have been free to make and the circumstances imposed upon me in which I had no choices to make. Only in this very qualified fashion could I accept Sartre's statement that "we are our choices"; yes, we are our choices, and we are also all the choices we did not get to make.

Essay # 4: "*Sartre's Philosophy*"

Sartre is right. Many of the choices we make do influence our lives. I am a living example of that. I chose to leave home at sixteen and support myself instead of letting my parents support me. I wanted to be independent and provide for myself. I got a job working as a switchboard operator at a hospital, and I moved in with my sister until I finished high school. By then I had enough money to have my own apartment. I got a scholarship to college because I had good grades in high school. Now I am majoring in nursing and hoping to be a registered nurse someday. If I could not make my own choices, I would not have been able to go out on my own, go to college, and become a nurse someday.

I think Sartre is right, we are our choices.

Essay #5: "Stick to Philosophy"

Jean-Paul Sartre is a philosopher, and only a philosopher could make a statement like "we are our choices" because philosophers deal in abstractions and life is not an abstraction.

I ate a pizza for dinner tonight. Did I choose to eat that pizza of my own free will, or was I influenced by the "Let Yourself Go" ad that Pizza Hut had on TV? A $30 million dollar a year advertising budget is enough to get anyone in there munching down pizza--are these people making choices or responding to Pavlovian conditioning?

If I can't even eat pizza of my own free will, how am I going to make the even bigger choices in life--like who am I going to be, what am I going to believe, what kind of lifestyle do I want, and how will I find personal fulfillment in life? Aren't I going to be batted around like some shuttlecock here, too? Aren't I going to decide it's neat to wear Polo shirts because of Ralph Lauren's multi-million dollar ad campaigns, and aren't I going to be influenced about being a sensitive male--like Alan Alda or Bill Cosby--or a macho brute, like Don Johnson or Sylvester Stallone, depending upon what image of the male my society approves of at any given moment? I'm probably going to be a pretty typical guy. I'm going to shave every morning or wear a beard (whatever's in vogue), put on the best-selling cologne, deodorant, and after-shave lotion, watch the Today show while I get dressed for work, grab up my copy of GQ to read on the bus, train, or subway to work, and the whole time think I am freely making choices and also free to make those choices.

C'mon, Mr. Sartre. Come into the real world. We're products of a media age--our lives are shaped, molded, defined, and packaged by commercial interests who have their pocketbooks and not our best interests in mind. We are our choices? Baloney. We're carbon copies of what the ad campaigns tell us to be. Even if we revolt, we do so in the most predictable ways--the punk rockers look alike, the druggies rot out their brains in search of elusive dreams, the motorcycle gangs have their own sense of "vogue" and what's "in" or "out." It's the same stuff, either way you cut it. Join in and wear your Guccis, or drop out and dye your Mohawk hairdo pink, purple, or green. Are these choices? No, these are people being manipulated into believing they have choices to make.

C'mon, Jean-Paul. I'll take you to Pizza Hut. We'll order a Deluxe pan pizza with everything on it and extra thick crust. We'll drink Classic Coke and watch big-screen MTV. Then we'll discuss this foolish idea you have about how we are our choices.

Group Exercise #2 enables you to see what works and what does not work well in an essay. It also enables you to see the significance of structure, or a logical plan of organization, to the value of an essay's achievement. Chances are that those essays rated superior by each group exhibited an organizational schema, while those essays that seemed like a random outpouring of ideas were rated poorly.

Information of this type should prove invaluable to you as you set about writing your assignments for your composition class and for other courses you are taking. Fundamental to improving your writing will be your own ability to assess whether your essay is organized in a fashion that reveals careful thought and a plan of development. Essays without such a plan generally wander from the topic and cause the reader to become impatient or confused.

One method for assessing the structure of your essay during its draft stages is to write in the margin beside each paragraph the main idea you are trying to communicate in that paragraph. If you cannot state the idea, that is a bad sign, for it tends to imply that the essay is poorly expressed and developed. If you find that you can state the ideas but that the order in which you have chosen to present the ideas does not make a great deal of sense, then the essay needs restructuring to make its ideas clearer and easier to follow.

An interesting method for looking carefully at your essay's structure is to photocopy your essay and then cut the essay apart with scissors, paragraph by paragraph. Now you have the structural components of your essay and can look at them more objectively as parts working together to form a whole.

First, try eliminating any of the paragraphs and see if anything has been lost. If you have an essay of ten paragraphs and you find that removing paragraph six has very little effect in terms of conveying meaning and making your ideas clear, then remove paragraph six because it is probably poorly located in the body of the text, extraneous, or repetitious.

Second, try rearranging the order of the paragraphs. Paragraph four really might go better after paragraph two than after paragraph three, and paragraph ten might not be your best ending but might work best as a middle paragraph of development. The possibilities for rearrangement are many, and you should take full advantage of them as you work on developing your drafts.

Many writers comment on the "first paragraph throw-away effect," a phenomenon common to both student and professional writers. In many instances, the first paragraph is really not all that essential to the essay and the true opening can be found in paragraph two, or in later paragraphs. The mind seems to be like an athlete who warms up before exercising, and very often the opening paragraph to many essays is a type of warm-up exercise before the mind gets down to the serious business of developing the assignment at hand. When looking at your essay for possibilities of revision before turning in your final draft, consider very carefully your opening paragraph to see if you really need it or not. Often you will find that you do not and that your essay begins (or formulates its thesis) much further along in the body of the text.

For example, consider this opening to an essay on the novels of John Steinbeck: "John Steinbeck's novels can be looked at from many points of view. A number of critics have argued that Steinbeck is a romantic writer, while others have viewed him as a realist. Others have argued that he is neither a romantic or a realist, but a populist. Considering Steinbeck's novels in terms of their complexity will enable us to see what a truly skilled and talented writer Steinbeck was."

The difficulty with this opening is that it says very little and gives the reader even less to focus upon. Exactly what will this essay be about and how will the author pursue developing a line of reasoning to support his or her views?

From this opening, it is impossible to tell what conclusions the writer will draw or what approach to Steinbeck's works will be taken. In truth, the writer is saying, "This is a complex issue that can be looked at in a number of ways." In another manner, the writer is indicating, "This topic is so vast and can be seen in so many ways that I hardly know where to begin except to state my confusion and draw it to the reader's attention."

Exercise #6

Review some of the papers that you have written for previous classes, either in high school or in college. Take a look at your openings and at the logical plan of development each paper offers. Based upon your analysis, critique your work and draw a profile of yourself as a writer, focusing upon strengths and weaknesses and also areas that you feel you have improved in or that still need additional work. How do you feel you have changed as a writer from these earlier papers until now? Based upon your own experience, what advice would you give to other writers on how to improve their work?

Point/Counterpoint: Considering Opposing Arguments

1. What does it mean to you to say that writing is a process and not a procedure? How do you define these two terms in relationship to writing? How would your view of writing change if you viewed it as a procedure? a process? Do you think this distinction is an important one? What does this distinction mean to you and your view of writing?

2. Do you feel that your textbook presents you with a view of writing as a procedure or a process? What evidence within the textbook leads you to this conclusion?

3. With a friend you discuss what you have been learning in your composition class, and she says to you, "I think the distinction being drawn between procedure and process is a meaningless one. A process is only a procedure with more variations and options." What would be your response to this statement?

4. Suppose there were two individuals who had two different views of how one goes about the act of writing. One believed that there are stages in the writing process, that these stages (like writing rituals and free writing) can be identified and defined, and that any one seeking to write who will go through these stages will learn to write and to write well. The other individual, however, believes that there is no one writing process but as many writing processes or methods as there are writers; that following other people's methods or processes in learning to write is no guarantee of success; and that writing, especially good writing, is not really linked up at all with identifiable stages or processes, but with a writer's interest in what he or she is writing about and a personal commitment, interest, and desire to express what he or she has to say clearly and well.

What types of discussions or debates could you imagine these two individuals getting into? What would be the largest philosophical issues dividing these two? Are there any aspects of their differing viewpoints that are reconcilable? Is there a side to this argument that you agree with more? Or is there another model or view of the writing process itself that you would propose?

SUMMARY AND ASSESSMENT PAGE

What ideas from *CHAPTER TWO: PURPOSE AND PROCESS FOR WRITING* (in either your textbook or your workbook) helped you the most with your writing? What ideas or techniques did you hope to get from this chapter but did not? What steps do you intend to take to learn those ideas or techniques?

"IT TAKES IMMENSE GENIUS TO REPRESENT,

SIMPLY AND SINCERELY, WHAT WE SEE IN FRONT OF US."

--EDMOND DURANTY

CHAPTER THREE: OBSERVING

Observation, or the act of recognizing and noting a fact or occurrence, is intrinsically related to the creative processes involved in writing. So, too, are the judgments or inferences to be drawn from what one has observed, and it is here that a great deal of the insight associated with observation resides.

Psychologist Rollo May considers the inferences to be drawn from observation as a type of intimate seeing that is unique and personal to each individual observer. He also describes this process as an involvement with and a penetration into reality that is invariably the starting point of creativity. As May states in "Creativity and Encounter":

Creativity occurs in an act of encounter, and is to be understood with this encounter at its center. Cezanne sees a tree. He sees it in a way no one else has ever seen it. He experiences, as he no doubt would say, a "being grasped" by the tree. The painting that issues out of this encounter between a person, Cezanne, and an objective reality, the tree, is literally new. Something is born, comes into being, something which did not exist before--which is as good a definition of creativity as we can get. Thereafter everyone who has the experience of encounter with the painting, who looks at it with intensity of awareness and lets it speak to him, will see the tree with the unique powerful movement and the architectural beauty which literally did not exist in our relation with trees until Cezanne experienced and painted them.

What May is describing is a type of experiential consciousness, or a consciousness that is keenly aware of its experiences and the possibilities they contain. Awareness of events, occurrences, and details, together with the ability to draw insightful inferences from this data, are what May identifies with the creative process.

Exercise #1

How would you relate May's concept of seeing and observing to the one presented to you by your textbook? Are they similar or dissimilar? Do they complement each other or contradict one another? Which of the two views of observing (May's or your textbook's) do you prefer and why?

Exercise #2

Your textbook states that "writing what you see helps you discover and learn more about your environment." Do you agree? Can you describe a situation or experience in which writing about what you saw helped you discover and learn more about your environment?

Exercise #3

Your textbook makes a distinction between objective and subjective seeing or observation. Choose an object or place and describe it both objectively and subjectively. What differences do you notice in these two approaches? How do these two approaches affect your writing, especially the "voice" or personal dimension of your writing?

Group Exercise #1

The teacher or a student selected for this exercise brings to class a cardboard box full of objects. The objects may come from the person's home or any number of locations, and they may be chosen at random or by design. The objects themselves are to be varied, but they may range from the most common and everyday, like a leaf, to the most unique and exotic.

On the day of the exercise, the person removes the objects from the box and places them on a desk or table for the class to see. The class will then write a descriptive essay about the items from the box that emphasizes both powers of observation and the ability to combine interesting musings or reflections upon the objects into an engaging, speculative essay.

The selection from Isak Dinesen's *Out of Africa* that tells of the death of the Iguana illustrates, by analogy, a great truth of descriptive writing. The writing must "pulse" with vitality and with an inner soul to radiate color and a sense of life. Otherwise, the writing will be flat and lifeless and will neither capture nor hold a reader's attention.

Dinesen's description also illustrates another truth of the writing process, that observation is the source of most written detail. What we observe and perceive we will bring to bear in our creativity and written expression. It would be impossible for us to do otherwise, since our recollections and our cognitive processes are intimately joined with our perceptions of our experiences in life.

The key to using observations well, though, is selectivity. We cannot write down every observation we have had throughout our lives, or every observation we have had about a particular subject, object, or topic. Putting down every impression we have, every thought, will make for a crowded and disorganized paper. Choosing selectively the details we do include will assure that we can achieve the types of effects and the dominant impression we are after.

Exercise #4

Here is another selection from Dinesen's *Out of Africa*. Consider the selection
in terms of its powers of description and its selective use of details. Is this a well-
written and effective description? What makes it so? What aspects of description,
like sensory details, comparisons and images, and describing what is *not* there, does
Dinesen use in this passage? How do these aspects work together in this passage to
create the passage's mood and its effects upon the reader?

There are times of great beauty on a coffee-farm. When the plantation flowered
in the beginning of the rains, it was a radiant sight, like a cloud of chalk, in the mist
and the drizzling rain, over six hundred acres of land. The coffee-blossom has a
delicate slightly bitter scent, like the blackthorn blossom. When the field reddened
with the ripe berries, all the women and the children, whom they call the Totos, were
called out to pick the coffee off the trees, together with the men; then the waggons
and carts brought it down to the factory near the river. Our machinery was never
quite what it should have been, but we had planned and built the factory ourselves
and thought highly of it. Once the whole factory burned down and had to be built up
again. The big coffee-dryer turned and turned, rumbling the coffee in its iron belly
with a sound like pebbles that are washed about on the sea-shore. Sometimes the
coffee would be dry, and ready to take out of the dryer, in the middle of the night.
That was a picturesque moment, with many hurricane lamps in the huge dark room of
the factory, that was hung everywhere with cobwebs and coffee-husks, and with
eager glowing dark faces, in the light of the lamps, round the dryer; the factory, you
felt, hung in the great African night like a bright jewel in an Ethiope's ear. Later on
the coffee was hulled, graded and sorted by hand, and packed in sacks sewn up with a
saddler's needle.

Then in the end in the early morning, while it was still dark, and I was lying in
bed, I heard the waggons, loaded high up with coffee-sacks, twelve to a ton, with
sixteen oxen to each waggon, starting on their way in to Nairobi railway station up
the long factory hill, with much shouting and rattling, the drivers running beside the
waggons. I was pleased to think that this was the only hill up, on their way, for the
farm was a thousand feet higher than the town of Nairobi. In the evening I walked
out to meet the procession that came back, the tired oxen hanging their heads in front
of the empty waggons, with a tired little Toto leading them, and the weary drivers
trailing their whips in the dust of the road. Now we had done what we could do. The
coffee would be on the sea in a day or two, and we could only hope for good luck in
the big auction-sales in London.

Exercise #5

Compare Dinesen's passage with the one that follows from Richard Selzer's *Mortal Lessons: Notes on the Art of Surgery.* In what ways are the descriptive techniques used by each author similar? In what ways do they differ? Which passage do you feel has greater power and effect? Why? Which passage makes a more striking use of imagery and vivid detail? In looking at these two passages, what have you learned about observing and about descriptive writing?

The patient is a young man recently returned from Guatemala, from the excavation of Mayan ruins. His left upper arm wears a gauze dressing which, when removed, reveals a clean punched-out hole the size of a dime. The tissues about the opening are swollen and tense. A thin brownish fluid lips the edge, and now and then a lazy drop of the overflow spills down the arm. An abscess, inadequately drained. I will enlarge the opening to allow better egress of the pus. . . .

No explorer ever stared in wilder surmise than I into that crater from which there now emerges a narrow gray head whose sole distinguishing feature is a pair of black pincers. The head stirs atop a longish flexible neck arching now this way, now that, testing the air. Alternately it folds back upon itself, then advances in new boldness. And all the while, with dreadful rhythmicity, the unspeakable pincers open and close. . . .

With all the ritual deliberation of a high priest I advance a surgical clamp toward the hole . . . . The rim achieved--now thrust--and the ratchets of the clamp close upon the empty air . . . . More stealth. Lying in wait . . . . Minutes pass, perhaps an hour . . . . A faint disturbance in the lake, and once again the thing upraises, farther and farther, hovering. Acrouch, strung, the surgeon is one with his instrument; there is no longer any boundary between its metal and his flesh. They are joined in a single perfect tool of extirpation. It is just for this that he was born. Now--thrust--and clamp--and *yes*. Got him!

Transmitted to the fingers comes the wild thrashing of the creature . . . . Tight grip now . . . steady, relentless pull. How it scrabbles to keep its tentacle-hold. With an abrupt moist plop the extraction is complete. There, writhing in the teeth of the clamp, is a dirty gray body, the size and shape of an English walnut. He is hung everywhere with tiny black hooklets. Quickly . . . into a specimen jar of saline . . . the lid screwed tight. Crazily he swims round and round, wiping his slimy head against the glass, then slowly sinks to the bottom, the mass of hooks in frantic agonal wave.

"You are going to be all right," I say to my patient. "We are *all* going to be all right from now on."

The next day I take the jar to the medical school. "That's the larva of the botfly," says a pathologist. "The fly usually bites a cow and deposits eggs beneath the skin. There, the egg develops into the larval form, which, when ready, burrows its way to the outside through the hide and falls to the ground. In time it matures into a full-grown botfly. This one happened to bite a man. It was about to come out on its own, and, of course, it would have died."

Selzer's essay is vividly descriptive and powerful in its impact. Obviously, a great deal of the essay's power comes from Selzer's keen attention to detail. This type of vivid accounting requires a minute observation of one's environment and an ability to select the most telling details for inclusion in the narrative.

Selzer, like Dinesen, was able to note and describe the details that caught his eye and held his attention. More importantly, he was able to elaborate these series of small details into a larger insight about the horror and shock to be found in unexpected encounters, particularly those involving human suffering and the odd juxtapositions of fate and circumstances.

Minus the very precise and accurate descriptions that denote a keen eye for detail, this passage would become much less effective and would function primarily as a narration of a series of events. Thus, it is safe to say that a fundamental principle of good descriptive writing is that the writer needs to be aware of his or her surroundings and aware of the details that make up individual experiences. Good descriptive writing begins with the keen observation of details.

Free Writing #1

Right now, wherever you are as you read this page, stop for a moment and look around you. Write down, on this page, the details of whatever you notice, whatever descriptive ideas, words, or phrases come to your mind. Jot down your ideas as quickly as they come, and strive for as complete a list of descriptive terms as you can create.

Free Writing #2

Try the same exercise as before of writing down descriptive details and phrases as they come to you, but, this time, let the focus of your writing be upon something from your memory, not an object or place immediately present to your eyes.

Exercise #6

Compare the two writing exercises, or free writings, that you have just completed. Which came more easily to you, the one that focused on your immediate surroundings, or the one you wrote from memory? Why do you think that might be?

Did you notice any difference in the way you felt as you were jotting down your ideas for these two writings? Did you find yourself more personally invested in the writing you did from memory than in the writing that described your immediate surroundings? Why do you think that might be? Do you think these two writing exercises might touch on the issues raised by the differences between objective and subjective descriptions? Why might that be?

Exercise #7

Excellent descriptive writings generally combine a keen eye for detail with an ability to draw interesting and insightful inferences from the details observed. Now it is your opportunity to combine these two aspects into the writing of an interesting essay.

Specifically, you are to (1) observe the details of a place or setting identified with the tastes or preferences of an individual and (2) draw inferences about what the person might be like, based upon the details you have observed.

A good example might be a student's dorm room, which often is decorated with posters, pictures, and memorabilia that say a great deal about what the student likes, values, and feels identified with. A keen observer could walk into that student's room, view these details, and draw inferences about what that student might be like as a person.

That is your assignment, to be that keen observer. Remember that the assignment has two parts, not only to observe details astutely, but to elaborate these details into a reasonable and reasoned inference about what these details might add up to and indicate about the person involved. Any setting to be observed is fine, as long as it allows you to fulfill the two parts of the assignment.

Here is another passage, this time from Donald Barthelme's short story, "The Sea of Hesitation," for you to consider for its descriptive effects.

I work for the City. In the Human Effort Administration. My work consists of processing applications. People apply for all sorts of things. I approve all applications and buck them upwards, where they are usually disapproved. Upstairs they do not agree with me, that people should be permitted to do what they want to do. Upstairs they have different ideas. But "different ideas" are welcomed, in my particular cosmos.

Before I worked for the City I was interested in changing behavior. I thought behavior could be changed. I had a B.A. in psychology, was working on an M.A. I was into sensory deprivation studies for a while at McGill and later at Princeton.

At McGill we inhabited the basement of Taub Hall, believed to be the first building in the world devoted exclusively to the study of hatred. But we were not studying hatred, we were doing black-box work and the hatred people kindly lent us their basement. I was in charge of the less intelligent subjects (the subjects were divided into less intelligent and more intelligent). I spent two years in the basement of Taub Hall and learned many interesting things.

The temperature of the head does not decrease in sleep. The temperature of the rest of the body does.

There I sat for weeks on end monitoring subjects who had half Ping-Pong balls taped over their eyes and a white-noise generator at 40db singing in their ears. I volunteered as a subject and, gratified at being assigned to the "more intelligent" group, spent many hours in the black box with half Ping-Pong balls taped over my eyes and the white-noise generator emitting its obliterating whine/whisper. Although I had some intricate Type 4 hallucinations, nothing much else happened to me. Except . . . I began to wonder if behavior *should be* changed. That there was "behavior" at all seemed to me a small miracle.

I pondered going on to stress theory, wherein one investigates the ways in which the stressed individual reacts to stress. but decided suddenly to do something else instead. I decided to take a job with the Human Effort Administration and to try, insofar as possible, to let people do what they want to do.

I am aware that my work is, in many ways, meaningless.

Barthelme's passage is fictional and differs from Dinesen's and Selzer's passages, which are based on actual experience; nonetheless, Barthelme's passage still indicates many of the aspects essential to good description based upon accurate observation, the effective use of details, and the types of inferences that can be drawn from these details.

Exercise #8

Do you agree that Barthelme's passage represents good descriptive writing? Why or why not? How do the details used in the passage contribute to its overall effects? What details stand out the most for you? Why do you think that might be? What issues about human existence does this passage raise? How are these issues communicated through the descriptive details Barthelme has chosen to include? If you had to infer from this passage what the person discussing his life might be like, what conclusions would you come to? Write out a portrait of this individual based upon the inferences and conclusions you have drawn.

Point/Counterpoint: Considering Opposing Arguments

1. Suppose an individual you met were to insist that the distinction made between objective and subjective description is an artificial one, since no act of description by an individual can ever exclude that individual's particular way of looking at, interpreting, and understanding the world; therefore, all description is, at its heart, subjective, even though it might appear to take on an objective surface or cast. How would you respond to this individual?

2. Do you consider the following selection from W. Somerset Maugham's *Rain* to be an example of subjective or objective description? Why?

She was a little woman, with brown, dull hair very elaborately arranged, and she had prominent blue eyes behind invisible pincenez. Her face was long, like a sheep's; but she gave no impression of foolishness, rather of extreme alertness; she had the quick movements of a bird. The most remarkable thing about her was her voice, high, metallic, and without inflection; it fell on the ear with a hard monotony, irritating to the nerves like the pitiless clamor of the pneumatic drill.

3. Your textbook states that "observing is essential to good writing." Do you agree? Do you think that this is true of *all* types of writing, or only descriptive writing?

4. Your textbook suggests a dichotomy between objective description, which depends upon accuracy and specific detail, and subjective description, which is directed more toward suggesting the value or relevance of what is being described. Apply this distinction to an analysis of the passages from Dinesen, Selzer, and Barthelme. In what ways do the authors of these passages use specific details to suggest values or relevance? What might be some of the values and insights the authors are suggesting through these passages?

5. Your textbook emphasizes that "describing what is *not* there" is an important aspect of observation and description. "Keen observation requires, sometimes, stepping back and noticing what is absent, what is not happening, who is not present." Do you agree? How would you apply this concept to the passages from Dinesen, Selzer, and Barthelme? Do you think it is truly possible to describe what is *not* there? Why might authors be interested in achieving this aim in their writings? What purpose would it serve in an observational piece to describe what is *not* there?

6. "What is seen depends on *who* is doing the seeing," your textbook states. What are you like as an observer? What aspects of a situation are you most likely to see, and which are you most likely to miss? Are there any biases or personal preferences associated with your seeing? What might these be, and how do they

affect your observational skills?

7. Return to the *Observing Objects* section of your textbook and reconsider the description by Paul Goldberger of the three types of cookies, the sugar wafer, the fig newton, and the mallomar. Goldberger elaborates a very complex analysis from these cookies that focuses upon their socio-political implications as man-made objects in the modern world. What do you think of Goldberger's analysis? Do you think it is perceptive or contrived? Do you think Goldberger has presented an interesting point of view that leads to greater insights, or do you feel he has overstated his case--that, for example, there are times when a cookie is only a cookie?

8. Your textbook states that spatial order and chronological order can be effective methods for organizing essays. Others might disagree, suggesting that these methods are too formulaic and predictable and therefore lead to dull, lackluster writing. Do you agree or disagree with this second view of organizing essays by spatial and/or chronological order?

9. You overhear this piece of conversation from a student who has just left a composition class that focused upon observational skills and descriptive writing: "Descriptive writing is an outdated skill. Nobody needs to describe anything in words anymore because we have modern technology, like cameras, tape recorders, and video-cameras, that can do descriptions much more thoroughly and accurately than trying to describe something in words. You know the old saying that one picture is worth a thousand words. Besides, describing something in words takes too much time? Why bother?"
How would you respond to this student?

SUMMARY AND ASSESSMENT PAGE

What ideas from *CHAPTER THREE: OBSERVING* (in either your textbook or your workbook) helped you the most with your writing? What ideas or techniques did you hope to get from this chapter but did not? What steps do you intend to take to learn those ideas or techniques?

"MEMORY IS THE MOTHER OF IMAGINATION, REASON AND SKILL . . . THIS IS THE COMPANION, THIS IS THE TUTOR, THE POET, THE LIBRARY WITH WHICH YOU TRAVEL."

--MARK VAN DOREN

CHAPTER FOUR: REMEMBERING

Here is a way to conceptualize the lasting and interesting effect memory has upon our lives. Think of a song that you have heard in two distinct time periods and phases of your life. Perhaps there was a love song that was very popular at the time you were graduating from high school that you heard again recently on the radio. Has your sense of that song changed now that you are older and no longer in love? Can you conceptualize two sets of memories surrounding that song, one set that involves happiness and fond memories because you were in love, and one set that brings back sad memories because of the loss of that love? Isn't it interesting that that one song can bring back both a happy and a poignant feeling as you hear it, and both of those feelings are representative of important moments and phases in your life?

This is the essence of memory. Not only does it enable us to recall very vivid and meaningful events in our lives, but it also allows us a double perspective upon those events. The Christmas song you associate with your family as a child will have a different meaning to you as you grow older and see your family in a new light. In the same manner, the song will take on even greater meaning when you have a family of your own and play that song for your children. Memory enables us to keep track of our lives and to be aware of the changes we have gone through in becoming who we are.

Free write about the ways that you might use memories to enhance your writing? What do you think it is about memories that adds a special and unique touch to writing, especially to descriptive writings and narration?

Group Exercise #1

Each person brings to class pictures of himself or herself at different points in life: perhaps a childhood photograph, a photograph from elementary or high school days, and a recent photograph. Each person will then write out an essay based upon what he or she was like in each of these photographs, each if these phases of life. How did the person in each of these photographs view life? What were the important issues surrounding his or her life at the time? What were some happy moments for this person, and some disappointments? How has his or her perspective on life changed from the earliest photograph to the most recent?

Let the class members hold up the photographs of themselves and share the memories associated with each phase. Let them address, too, the issue of: "If I knew then what I know now, I would have . . . " If the essays written about the photographs are not too intensely personal, let each person read out loud what he or she has written and share these reflections with the class.

Memory is more than a handy device to help you recall names and places, faces and dates. Memory is a highly valued intellectual skill, especially in our contemporary era of information processing in which there are vast amounts of material associated with almost any profession one might choose. Beyond memory's practical value, it is also a highly cherished aspect of our individual identities, since our personal experiences, and the unique way we recall them, are at the heart of our uniqueness as individuals.

The concept of memory has a long and noble tradition. Memory (*memoria* in Latin and *mneme* in Greek) was considered one of the five essential elements for rhetoric during the classical period. The other four elements included *invention*, or the ability to conceptualize ideas; *arrangement*, or what we commonly mean today by the concept of an essay's organization; *style*, or the sophistication of one's language use, which includes vocabulary, sentence structure, and sentence variety; and *delivery*, since, in ancient Greece and Rome, compositions were delivered orally. Today a more inclusive term would be *presentation*, which would allow for both oral and written forms.

Quintilian, a Roman rhetorician who wrote in the first century A.D., described memory as the "treasury" of invention, and informed his students that it was important "to learn much by heart and to think much, and if possible, to do this daily, since there is nothing that is more increased by practice or impaired by neglect than memory . . . . For our whole education depends on memory" and "it is the power of memory alone that brings before us all the store of precedents, laws, rulings, sayings and facts which the orator must possess in abundance."

The value and importance of memory were confirmed by St. Augustine (354-430 A.D.), who defined a view of memory that continued into the medieval period and that still has a popular influence today in theories of cognition and intellectual development. Augustine thought of memory as part of each person's inner experiences, which included memory, intellect, and will. These three functions, working together, comprised human consciousness. The intellect contemplated both present experience and the recollections (or memory) of past experience and then directed the will to act upon the intellect's viewpoints or conclusions.

Stated another way, Augustine believed that the individual remembers what he or she is doing in every act; understands or knows his or her immediate experience; and can will to act or not to act, based upon what he or she knows and remembers. To Augustine, the three aspects of the human soul (or personality) described as memory, intellect, and will created the sources of ideas, judgment, and actions. These three functions also generated the corresponding activities of being, knowing, and willing.

Exercise #1

The classical rhetoricians and St. Augustine both viewed memory as an integrated aspect of human consciousness, or part of what created the uniqueness of each individual's personal legacy of existence in the world. Do you agree with this view? Do you feel that memory is truly a part of what gives you your unique identity as an individual? How do you personally feel memory relates to other aspects of your life, such as choosing a course of action or knowing what is "true" for you as an individual?

Contemporary theorists tend to divide memory into three components, *skill*, *verbal response*, and *emotional response*. *Skill* involves our ability to recall what we have learned to do, like ride a bicycle, for example. We may learn this skill in June and apply it again in July. We are able to do this because we can remember the skill that we have learned. If we were unable to do this, we would have to re-learn *everything* each time we wanted to do something! A monumental and time-consuming task, at best.

Verbal response is what most of us generally think of when we consider memory, for *verbal response* involves the ability to recall a specific event or idea, like who was the first president of the United States, what date and time our next appointment is with the dentist, what recipe to follow in making lasagna, etc. This aspect of memory, like the ability to recall a *skill*, is one that can be improved through concentration, practice, and the use of certain techniques to aid recall.

Emotional response, however, as the name suggests, involves our feelings about certain events or experiences. A person, for example, might learn to be afraid of snakes, and that fear can stay with the person for all of his or her life--far beyond the duration of the first immediate encounter with the snake itself.

Some skills, verbal responses, and emotional responses stay with a person throughout his or her lifetime. Others are forgotten over time. Many psychologists feel that verbal responses usually are more easily forgotten than skills and emotional responses. They also endorse the view (similar to St. Augustine's) that memory is connected with every mental process, every emotion, and every impression received through the senses. A person may remember the taste of a lemon, the scent of a rose, a line from a poem. He or she may also remember the joy felt at making a new friend or receiving the most wonderful present ever dreamed of one snowy Christmas Eve.

Exercise #2

Another way of rephrasing what contemporary theorists say about memory is to say that we learn to do (skill), to say (verbal response), and to feel (emotional response). Obviously, this gives a very large and important role to memory in our lives, since it affects every aspect of our consciousness.

Do you agree with this perspective, or would you assign memory to a less important role in human affairs? Do you agree that emotional responses stay with a person longer than verbal responses? Why might that be? What role do you feel memory has played in your learning? What role has it played in your writing?

Exercise #3

When Quintilian described memory as the "treasury" or treasure house of rhetoric (the uses of language), most likely he had in mind the types of memories we now associate with emotional responses. From a person's recollection of feelings and of the events and associations related to those feelings comes a rich "treasury" of ideas the person can draw upon for communicating with others. Do you agree with this view of memory? What role do you feel this view of memory plays in your writing?

Group Exercise #2

Leslie Marmon Silko, a contemporary American Indian writer, describes memory in this fashion in her novel, *Ceremony*:

> Ts'its'tsi'nako, Thought-Woman,
>   is sitting in her room
> and whatever she thinks about
>   appears.
>
> She thought of her sisters,

Nau'ts'ity'i and I'tcts'ity'i,
and together they created the Universe
this world
and the four worlds below.

Thought-Woman, the spider,
named things and
as she named them
they appeared.

She is sitting in her room
thinking of a story now.

I'm telling you the story
she is thinking.

Let the class form itself into groups of four or five students each. One student
in each group will serve as Thought-Woman, or the source of memory and ideas.
This student will write down a word or idea that comes to mind, like *apple* or
disappointment; or *how to end an argument with a friend*.

The student will then share what he or she has written down with each person in
the group. On separate sheets of paper, each person in the group will write down
what comes to his or her mind in relationship to the the original idea.

Each group is to do this exercise for at least ten concepts or ideas provided to
them by Thought-Woman. At the end of this part of the exercise, the group will
consider the information it has gathered on the ideas it has explored under Thought-
Woman's direction.

For the final part of the exercise, the separate ideas and musings are to be
combined into a commentary or narrative upon the original idea or concept presented
to the group. This final act of bringing the separate sets of ideas together into a
composite narrative can be done by Thought-Woman, or by the group as a whole. It
will be important, too, for the group to reflect upon the process of creating ideas from
memory that has just occurred, as well as to evaluate and critique the significance
and implications of the composite narrative produced by the group.

Exercise #4

What significance do you find in the fact that Silko calls Thought-Woman "the
spider?" Do you think that she is suggesting that there is a "web-like" quality to
memory, in that memory is like a web of associations and one idea remembered can
"shake the web" and set off a series of related memories and recollections? Do you
feel this is a perceptive view of memory? Has this view been true of your

experiences? Do you find this is the process that occurs in your writing, too, when you write from memory? Why do you think that might be?

In the *Prologue* to *The Way to Rainy Mountain*, N. Scott Momaday writes:

The journey herein recalled continues to be made anew each time the miracle comes to mind, for that is peculiarly the right and responsibility of the imagination. It is a whole journey, intricate with motion and meaning; and it is made with the whole memory, that experience of the mind which is legendary as well as historical, personal as well as cultural. And the journey is an evocation of three things in particular: a landscape that is incomparable, a time that is gone forever, and the human spirit, which endures. The imaginative experience and the historical express equally the traditions of man's reality. Finally, then, the journey recalled is among other things the revelation of one way in which these traditions are conceived, developed, and interfused in the human mind.

Exercise #5

Momaday's view of memory involves the legendary, the historical, the cultural, and the personal. Discuss what you think he might mean by these concepts. How would you envision memory as being affected by these four concepts? Can you envision ways in which the historical and cultural aspects of memory might conflict with the personal aspects? Why do you think that might be? What do you think might be the end result of such a conflict?

Exercise #6

In the previously quoted passage, Momaday makes a clear connection between memory and the imagination. Do you think that memory and imagination are integrally related? Why? Can the imagination function without memory? Can memory function without imagination? What would be your own definition of the imagination?

Exercise #7

In the previous passage, Momaday expresses, too, a deep respect for the land (landscape) and its influence upon memory and imagination. Further in his book, he also states: "I came to know that country, not in the way a traveler knows the landmarks he sees in the distance, but more truly and intimately, in every season, from a thousand points of view. . . .Once in his life a man ought to concentrate his mind upon the remembered earth, I believe. He ought to give himself up to a particular landscape in his experience, to look at it from as many angles as he can, to wonder about it, to dwell upon it."

Is there a particular place (or landscape) that you feel a strong attachment to, the kind of empathy and respect that Momaday describes for his landscape? Why do you feel you might have such a strong attachment to that place? Is the actual place different from the landscape of the place you have created in your mind? Why do you think that might be?

How would you describe this place to another person in such a way that he or she could sense and feel the emotional pull this place had upon your life and memory? Do you think some people are more affected by a sense of place than others are? Why do you think that might be?

Free Writing #2

Now try writing about your sense of a landscape, a place, as a free writing. Is there a shift in your focus or feelings in writing about this topic as a free writing? Does the use of a free writing here enable you to be more personal and self-disclosing with your "voice" in writing about a landscape that has meaning for you than a piece of writing, as essay, directed toward an audience? Why do you think that might be?

Students sometimes indicate that writing from memory seems to them an overwhelming task, largely because they are called upon to supply the data and materials for their writing. They prefer, instead, assignments in which the materials are given to them and they can respond.

Actually, though, writing from memory is not very much different from the processes involved in other types of writing. It requires a clear sense of your primary focus, or the main idea you wish to communicate, and a sense of an organizational schema. More importantly, writing from memory, like all forms of writing, requires a sense of purpose, or the *reason* why you are writing the essay. Do you wish to persuade your reader that the house you grew up in was the most beautiful house in the most peaceful of rustic neighborhoods? Do you wish to reminisce and share your fondly remembered feelings? Do you hope that writing about your memories will give your readers insights into your experience and a certain sense of the universality of all human experience? All of these concerns form your purpose in writing, and it is your purpose that will give form, power, and impact to your writing and also enable you to adopt the "voice" you wish to entertain, persuade, share with, or enlighten your audience. Until you are certain of your reason for writing, your purpose, your work will stay nebulous and unclear. You may feel the frustration of not knowing where to begin or what to say, together with the disheartening experience of many starts and stops--the discouraging realization that one student describes as "a pile of wadded up papers growing higher and higher on the floor." With purpose, your writing takes on a focus and a clarity that make for significance and grace in your essay.

Consider the following selection from Maya Angelou's autobiography, *I Know Why the Caged Bird Sings*. Author and poet, Angelou grew up in Stamps, Arkansas and was raised by her grandmother (who is referred to in the selection as Sister Henderson). With her brother Bailey and her Uncle Willie, Angelou lived in the back of her grandmother's country store, which she describes as her "favorite place to be." As you read the selection, think about what might be Angelou's purpose in writing about this country store in Stamps, Arkansas, a long time ago, when she was just a child.

Weighing the half-pounds of flour, excluding the scoop, and depositing them dust-free into the thin paper sacks held a simple kind of adventure for me. I developed an eye for measuring how full a silver-looking ladle of flour, mash, meal, sugar or corn had to be to push the scale indicator over to eight ounces or one pound. When I was absolutely accurate our appreciative customers used to admire: "Sister Henderson sure got some smart grandchildrens." If I was off in the Store's favor, the eagle-eyed women would say, "put some more in that sack, child. Don't you try to make your profit offa me."

Then I would quietly but persistently punish myself. For every bad judgment, the fine was no silver-wrapped Kisses, the sweet chocolate drops that I loved more than anything in the world, except Bailey. And maybe canned pineapples. My obsession with pineapples nearly drove me mad. I dreamt of the days when I would be grown and able to buy a whole carton for myself alone.

Although my syrupy golden rings sat in their exotic cans on our shelves year round, we only tasted them during Christmas. Momma used the juice to make almost-black fruit cakes. Then she lined heavy soot-encrusted iron skillets with the pineapple rings for rich upside-down cakes. Bailey and I received one slice each, and I carried mine around for hours, shredding off the fruit until nothing was left except the perfume on my fingers. I'd like to think that my desire for pineapples was so sacred that I wouldn't allow myself to steal a can (which was possible) and eat it alone out in the garden, but I'm certain that I must have weighed the possibility of the scent exposing me and didn't have the nerve to attempt it.

Until I was thirteen and left Arkansas for good, the Store was my favorite place to be. Alone and empty in the mornings, it looked like an unopened present from a stranger. Opening the front doors was pulling the ribbon off the unexpected gift. The light would come in softly (we faced north), easing itself over the shelves of mackerel, salmon, tobacco, thread. It fell flat on the big vat of lard and by noontime during the summer the grease had softened to a thick soup. Whenever I walked into the Store in the afternoon, I sensed that it was tired. I alone could hear the slow pulse of its job half done. But just before bedtime, after numerous people had walked in and out, had argued over their bills, or joked about their neighbors, or just dropped in "to give Sister Henderson a 'Hi y'all,'" the promise of magic mornings returned to the Store and spread itself over the family in washed life waves.

Exercise #8

What do you think Angelou's purpose might be in writing this description? How does memory work within the context of this piece? What do Angelou's recollections of life in the Store and with her family add to this work? How is this work influenced by the fact that Angelou is an adult recalling a childhood experience? Which perspective do you feel she adopts in narrating this piece, that of the child, or of the adult? What aspects of this piece make it an effective recollection? What values and attitudes does Angelou describe for herself, her grandmother (Sister Henderson), and for the townspeople? How do these attitudes and values contribute to the effect of the piece? What is the underlying organizational principle to this piece when Angelou describes the Store and the people it serves? What type of mood or feeling does Angelou convey to you about the Store and her life in Stamps, Arkansas?

Writing about remembered places, people, or events might seem difficult, but some general principles do apply when you are using the "treasury" of memory as the source for your essays. Writing from memory always involves the creation of a vivid scene, whether that scene focuses upon a place, an event, or the people living in he place and contributing to the event. Scenes in such descriptions cannot be vague or generalized, but must depend upon precise, detailed, and vivid imagery to convey their meaning to a reader.

Think of what a poor description Angelou would have written if she had described her Store in terms that would have fit any or all stores anywhere in the world. Instead, she filled her recollection with personal meanings, associations, and treasured viewpoints to give power to her work and to captivate her readers.

While visual images predominate in Angelou's description, you will notice, too, how effectively she uses appeals to the senses of hearing, smell, touch, and taste to convey her ideas. Beyond that, she uses comparisons, metaphors, and similes. The piece is filled with an evocative use of figurative language, like the "thick soup" of the lard melting on a hot summer afternoon, or the view of the Store as "an unopened present from a stranger." Consider the grace and beauty in the description of the Store in the late evenings, when "the promise of magic mornings returned . . . and spread itself over the family in washed life waves." All of the imagistic uses of language in the piece contribute to creating in the reader's mind the vivid scene that was the Store for Angelou.

In addition to vivid imagery and detailed descriptions, a piece written from memory needs a clear indication of the memory's significance. Usually the significance is found in the personal feelings, associations, and insights the writer feels about what person, place, or event is being remembered. Thus, to write well about a memory that has personal significance requires a degree of self-disclosure. To reveal both memories and feelings, to share one's insights, perspectives, and values, are all important aspects of writing well from memory.

All of these factors lead to some guidelines for writing well from memory. The first and most important consideration is if you remember the person, place, or event well enough to present a clear and vivid image of it to the reader.

The second concern focuses upon your willingness to be self-disclosing and self-revealing with your readers. It is not always easy to share one's inner feelings, particularly if they are painful, or tinged with disappointment, or have the potential to present us in less than an ideal light, but this capacity for self-disclosure is at the heart of writing from memory.

The third consideration is the universality of your experience, or the issue of whether your essay will lead your readers to reflect upon their own experiences and upon human life in general. For example, you might recall vividly the day you got your first bicycle, but if you write only of the events and details that surround that incident, filling your work with specifics of interest more to you than to anyone else, you will probably write a relatively unengaging piece.

If, however, you see in your description the potential to reveal insights about a child's sense of wonder and delight in the world, or the fused joys and fears in having to learn a new skill like riding a bicycle for the first time, or the tenderness and love of parents who make sacrifices so that their children's wishes can come true, then you have a greater chance of producing an essay that will engage your readers fully.

Point/Counterpoint: Considering Opposing Arguments

1. Do you feel that writing from memory is important? Why? How would you respond to a person who views writing from memory only as self-indulgent and overly emotional?

2. Two students leave a composition class in which the teacher has just given an assignment to write an essay about a favorite person, place, or event in one's life. Andrew turns to Sarah and says, "You know, I hate this assignment. I think my memories are personal and private and that I shouldn't have to share them with anyone if I don't want to. Besides, what's the big deal? How can my memories have any meaning to someone else who wasn't there to begin with?"
    If you were Sarah, how would you respond to Andrew's objections?

3. Your textbook states that *voice* "refers to a writer's personality as revealed through language" and suggests that the "personal voice," which is very much about human feelings and emotions, is often the most appropriate one for writing from memory. Ben and Tom have just left the same composition class as Andrew and Sarah. Ben says to Tom, "I don't see the value of all this emphasis upon a 'personal voice' in writing. That's all well and good for people who are going to be creative writers, but what about people like me? I'm going to be an engineer, and the odds that I'll ever need to use a 'personal voice' in my writing are slim to none. I'm *sure* I'll never have to use a 'personal voice' to write from memory in my career. I feel like I'm wasting my time. What I need to learn is the type of *impersonal* tone or voice that will give my professional writing an air of scientific objectivity."
    How would you respond to Ben's objections?

4. Lauren and Michelle, students in the same class, are discussing the assignment, and Lauren says, "I am hesitant to write from memory, and I don't even know if it's a good idea. I know my memory is not all that accurate. I can remember some things well, but not others. How do I know when I write this assignment that I won't distort what I remember, or leave out important details, or idealize the people and places I remember because they mean so much to me? How can I know I can trust my memory to be accurate and not distorted, too?"
    How would you respond to Lauren's objections?

5. Write an essay about a significant event in your life. Choose an event that will interest your reader and, at the same time, reveal an aspect of yourself and your views. After you have completed the essay, write it again but from a more objective viewpoint, as if you were a journalist recounting another person's story. Compare the two essays. What differences do you note in voice, tone, organization, and effect? Which essay to you seems the more effective? Which essay do you prefer? Why?

6. The essay on trash day by Kurt Weekly presented in your textbook illustrates one view of the value of writing about remembered events: often this process can have a cathartic effect, relieving people of pent-up emotions and frustrations and freeing them from the pain of unresolved emotional conflicts. Often clients in therapy are encouraged to write from their memories, keeping a journal of the events that have shaped their personalities and a record of their changing perspectives about their life experiences.

Do you agree with this perspective of the value of writing about remembered events? Have you ever found it of value in your own life? Do you believe that writing about a remembered event might give a person an opportunity to make touch with the deepest of "inner voices" and write honestly about an experience that might have been problematic? Do you feel that memories *are* the "inner voice" within a person? Why do you think that might be?

7. Your textbook emphasizes dialogue as one aspect of writing about remembered events. Maya Angelou incorporates a small amount of dialogue into her description of life in the Store. How do you feel her essay would have changed if more dialogue had been included? Do you think it would have made the essay stronger or weaker to include more dialogue? Why?

8. Swiss psychologist Carl Jung (1875-1961) theorized that memory was both individual and "collective." Jung believed that all memory resided in the unconscious mind and was composed of (1) uniquely individual recollections based upon a person's life experiences and (2) a "collective unconscious" comprised of a historical memory that all individuals participate in. From this "collective" memory (or "collective unconscious") derive the archetypes, or mythological patterns, that are repeated across cultures and across historical eras as part of each group's religious and cultural value patterns.

Research Jung's theories and apply them to your own views of memory. Do you agree or disagree with Jung's perspective?

SUMMARY AND ASSESSMENT PAGE

What ideas from *CHAPTER FOUR: REMEMBERING* (in either your textbook or your workbook) helped you the most with your writing? What ideas or techniques did you hope to get from this chapter but did not? What steps do you intend to take to learn those ideas or techniques?

"THE LANGUAGE LEADS,

AND WE CONTINUE TO FOLLOW WHERE IT LEADS"

--WRIGHT MORRIS

CHAPTER FIVE: INVESTIGATING

Your textbook suggests that investigation begins with questions to uncover truths not generally known or accepted. In the process of investigating, you (1) discover facts; (2) report those facts to other people who need to know; (3) explain the causes of the facts in detail; (4) evaluate the facts and events; (5) offer a solution; and (6) persuade your readers to a certain belief or course of action. Your main purpose in investigating a topic is to organize and report information clearly in such a way that your readers will find interesting and accessible.

While reporting information might seem like an easy writing task, many writers often find it a challenging one because of the premium it places upon locating one's thesis clearly and then determining what supporting points to include or exclude. Central to good investigative writing is determining exactly how much your audience already knows about a topic so that the information you give them is relevant and new. If you bore your audience by repeating information they already know, you lose the audience engagement essential to clear communication. On the other hand, if you exclude important information, you run the risk of confusing your audience and also disrupting the communication process. Navigating carefully between these two extremes is an important aspect of reporting information clearly and well.

Free Writing #1

Free write for ten or fifteen minutes about your own processes of investigating and finding out facts. Perhaps you could write about, too, a time in your life when you investigated and researched information in order to make an informed decision. How did your investigative processes help with clarifying your decision-making processes?

Essays reporting information share certain features in common. For one, obviously, they have a thesis they wish to present to an audience, as well as an interesting slant taken toward their subjects. Like all essays, the thesis in an informative essay must be narrowed so that the topic is not so broad that an audience is overwhelmed with information and cannot follow what is being discussed.

Second, a good informative essay requires an appeal to the reader's interests. If you are writing about molecular biology to a general, lay audience with little knowledge of biology, you cannot write your piece with a wealth of terminology, facts, and statistics that only people trained in biology would understand. Finding the audience's interests involves finding a way of making the material relevant to an audience's need for the information. What about molecular biology will influence my audience's lives? What is the value of the information I have to share with them? How can I best convey the significance of the information I have discovered?

Third, informative essays must clearly define any technical terms used. Often the language used to discuss certain topics is highly specialized and technical; some might even say jargonized. If you are writing about the mining industry and black lung disease and you use the term *alveoli*, it will be very important that you clarify for a general audience that you are discussing air sacs in the lungs. Without this definition, there is the potential that a great deal of what you are discussing will be lost to your audience.

The concept of defining your terms applies not only to specialized vocabularies but to commonly used words as well. If you are writing an essay on justice, for example, it is not always safe to assume that both you and your audience share the same definition of justice. It would be wise for you to define your view of justice and then center your essay around that definition. And here is an important point to remember, too. Always remain consistent throughout your essay with the definition you have chosen. Do not shift terms or definitions. That is, do not define justice in one way in paragraph two and then use another definition in paragraph five. Your essay will be weak and logically inconsistent if you do, and the points you wish to make will not be clear.

The fourth point to remember is that an informative essay must reveal an underlying logical plan of organization. Facts and details thrown at a reader in a relatively random fashion will not be very interesting or convincing. Facts marshalled together toward a central point will be. Often investigative essays provide a great wealth of information and a large number of details. To be effective, investigative essays must divide the information into categories that make sense and that support the main thesis. Divisions suggest, too, that transitions amongst the divisions must be clear in order to tie all the information together and to indicate a clear sense of flow to the ideas.

Often when one has worked on an investigative piece for a long time, the information seems very clear simply because of the amount of exposure the writer has had to the material. Never forget, though, that your reader will be taking the information in for the first time, and often what seems so crystal clear to you will not be very clear to your reader unless you organize well and give lots of signals about the transitions amongst ideas that you are making. Leave nothing to chance, and cover all your bases. That way you will avoid a whole range of possible misinterpretations that can obscure your message and negate all your hard work.

One of the most common methods for organizing investigative essays is the use of narrative examples. Examples illustrate or reinforce an idea that is being expressed, and often they can clarify a point better than any other rhetorical technique. People like stories, and generally they grasp a visual concept more quickly and clearly than they do a verbally defined one.

If you doubt that this is true, watch the audience next time you hear a speaker present a talk. Watch how the level of interest rises when the speaker says, "Let me tell you a story," or, "Let me illustrate my point with an example." Of course the clearest proof of this concept is the parable, a teaching technique used throughout the Bible to illustrate complex metaphysical and spiritual ideas through the use of stories that illustrate the key idea. Humanity's relationship to God is a difficult concept to communicate to an audience, but the idea of a good and caring shepherd going out in search of his lost sheep makes this idea all the easier to grasp.

Remember, too, that an idea visually illustrated through an example stays in the audience's mind a lot longer than ideas illustrated through facts, statistics, or long verbal descriptions and definitions. A good rule is to back up and support your verbal descriptions with the careful placing of illustrative examples. Aim for a good mix of the two to produce a rhetorically convincing essay.

It is important, though, that we are perfectly clear on what is meant by an example. Students often mistake the statement of a personal preference for an example in writing such statements as: "Computers are the most important technological advance since the development of electricity. For example, computer programs that do spelling checks and stylistic analysis are my favorites because they make writing essays so much easier. Nobody who has ever used a computer could argue against the view of how important computers have been to making the contemporary era better for mankind."

The writer of the opening to this essay on computers has failed to realize that examples are designed to illustrate a larger point. Simply writing "for example" does not make the statement that follows a true example. It is important to remember, too, that your examples must be relevant in supporting the main point (or thesis) of the paragraph. Otherwise the example is wasted and extraneous, as in the following excerpt from a student paper: "The cosmetic industry in America has redefined beauty in our culture, moving us away from an appreciation of natural beauty and toward a near worship of artificial glamour. The result is a further entrenchment in our culture of the idea that superficial values are the most important measures of a woman's worth. For example, women now have foundation to choose from, mascara, concealers, eye shadow, eye liners, blush, lipsticks, tinted contact lenses. Where does it all end?"

The topic of this paragraph requires an example of how the cosmetic industry reinforces the idea of superficial values in our culture's assessment of women, yet the example itself does not directly address this point but only lists the types of cosmetics that are available to women. The example is close to the mark, but not exactly on it. The essay itself would be more cohesive if the example were used later in the paper to illustrate the types of choices available to women, in cosmetics, that can alter their natural appearances and make them mimic more closely a cultural ideal of femininity and of female beauty. The guideline here to follow, as in the use of all examples, is to establish a clear connection between your example and the point being made in your essay.

Exercise #1

Choosing effective examples and using them well in your compositions is an interesting rhetorical challenge. Support or negate each of the following statements with at least three appropriate examples. Make sure your examples are relevant to the thesis and not only peripherally related to the main idea.

1. A college education is a prerequisite for success in today's world.

2. Fraternities and sororities encourage elitism.

3. They don't make cars like they used to.

4. Contemporary rock music is lousy because the lyrics are no good; they have nothing to say.

5. What we call "love" is an illusion; it comes and goes like the wind.

6. UFO's are a hoax.

7. Government officials are corrupt.

8. The fine arts are only for elitists and intellectuals.

9. People will cheat to get ahead these days.

10. Technology enhances people's lives.

Investigative writing is often involved with giving a step-by-step explanation of a process. The explanations may involve micro-processes (or the steps involved in accomplishing a specific task, such as baking a cake or changing a tire on a car), or macro-processes, which involve abstract philosophical issues like how socio-economic status affects voting patterns, or how religious faith influenced the art of the medieval period. Each type of explanation of process involves different investigative strategies and different philosophical approaches, but both necessitate a keen eye for detail and an ability to draw clear inferences.

In many ways, the descriptive and observational writing you have been working on in previous chapters will serve you well in your investigative writing because many of the strategies apply equally as well. Since all writing involves the application of critical thinking skills, you will find as you work on your writing that the skills intertwine--that is, a skill you learn for descriptive writing will serve you well in investigative writing, logical analysis, narration by example, and a host of other writing techniques. In essence, skills build upon each other and compound over time, so no skill has a single or exclusive use that cannot be applied in other writing situations. In fact, think of all your skills coming together to create a myriad of effects in a range of writing situations. This fact is part of the reason writing is viewed as both a process and an art.

Exercise #2

If you were assigned the task of investigating your own writing, processes, how would you go about it? In other words, what steps would you follow to investigate the micro-processes and macro-processes involved in how you write?

Many students fail to realize in investigative writing that investigative writing is itself a process in which a series of basic steps can be followed. First and foremost, begin with a clear statement of purpose. Tell your reader what topic you are investigating and how you propose to pursue your investigation.

Of course, you will want to show a greater degree of finesse with your style than simply saying: "In this paper, I will be investigating the causes teenage delinquency, and I will be basing my analysis upon interviews with social workers, library research, and statistical analyses of data I have accumulated from a questionnaire I designed and administered." Such an opening would be too formulaic and uninteresting.

What you would need, instead, would be a sentence or two of background information (exposition) and then a statement of your purpose: "Teenage delinquency has been a major social problem in America for the last three decades. Despite the efforts of government agencies to address the problem through social work and job-training programs, teenage delinquency has continued to rise. A range of solutions has been proposed, and one of the most important issues facing society today is to determine which of these approaches will be the most effective in lowering the crime rate amongst juveniles."

Be sure that you know the process you are investigating. This seems a simple (perhaps too simple) point, but it you would be surprised how many students tackle the investigation of processes they do not fully understand. Remember, you do not need to know the process in detail *before* you begin your investigation, but you must know it in detail by the time you translate your knowledge to the written page for your reader.

If the process you are investigating, or the process of your investigation, can be broken down into steps, make sure that the details of each individual step are clear and complete so that you avoid confusing your reader. Similarly, to avoid confusion, be sure you indicate through transitions when and how you are moving from one point to another. The least preferred way of accomplishing this is a technique known as listing, or a simple enumeration of points: "first, second, third . . . , etc." For most essays--as opposed to business reports and technical writing where this technique is highly prized--such listing of points is again too formulaic and too indicative of a lack of sophisticated strategies for organizing one's materials. Smoother transitions generally read better and give your essay a measure of polish.

One teacher encourages her students to think of this aspect of writing as similar to a magic act. Magic only works if you do not notice the "tricks" the magician is pulling. The fact that you cannot see what the magician is doing, only the results, is was makes magic so magical. Imagine if the magician were to come out before his act and say, "I am now going to remove a rabbit from my hat. I am going to have the rabbit in the false bottom of the hat, and, as I place my hand in the hat, I will lift the false bottom off and remove the rabbit. Then, to make him disappear again, I will place my hand in the hat, put the rabbit in the false bottom, and slip the top over him. Now watch my act as I perform it for you."

The odds are that you would be profoundly bored by such an introduction and not the least bit impressed by the trick because you would be aware of every motion and of what was coming next. In a similar vein, think of going to someone's house for dinner and having him or her say, "I am now going to serve the salad. I will place the salad bowl in the middle of the table and the individual serving bowls by your plates. When the salad bowl is in place, you may serve yourselves by passing the salad bowl in a clockwise fashion around the table. When all have been served, replace the salad bowl in the center of the table."

You would probably be inclined to say, "Forget the talk. Just serve the salad!"

While this description is humorous, it still points out an important issue with regard to writing. The more you call attention to what you are doing in writing through formulas like lists or through excessively formal introduction and transitions like, "In this paper I will discuss the three aspects of neo-Freudian psychology that have had the most pronounced effect upon contemporary theories of personality integration. The first aspect of neo-Freudian psychology I am going to discuss is . . .," the more you make your paper about as interesting and artistic as an overly explained magic act or dinner party.

This exercise is an investigation of transitions and how they work in writing. Like all investigations, it involves the gathering and interpretation of data.

Each person will bring to class three selections from writings he or she admires. The class will divide into groups and discuss each selection, paying particular attention to the issues of overly formal introductions and of transitions amongst ideas. The groups will then prepare a general assessment or guideline for determining the effectiveness of transitions in writing. The essay that exhibits the best transitions, in the group's opinion, will be presented and discussed as a model for the class to study and learn from in the process of developing their own sense of how to write effective transitions.

Sometimes in writing a paper it is easy to become "stuck" and to want to fall back on old ways of writing that seem familiar and safe. For some writers, this impulse is so strong that they never even entertain the notion of trying anything new--which is the equivalent of saying they never open themselves up to new learning. Since we are discussing investigative papers, now is the time to do an investigation of how you can avoid falling back on old ways and structuring essays in the most formulaic of fashions. Consider the method that writer Isaac Asimov suggests in the essay, "The Eureka Phenomenon":

It is my belief, you see, that thinking is a double phenomenon, like breathing.

You can control breathing by deliberate voluntary action: you can breathe deeply and quickly, or you can hold your breath altogether, regardless of the body's needs at the time. This, however, doesn't work well for very long. Your chest muscles grow tired your body clamors for more oxygen, or less, and you relax. The automatic involuntary control of breathing takes over, adjusts it to the body's needs, and unless you have some respiratory disorder, you can forget about the whole thing.

Well, you can think by deliberate voluntary action, too, and I don't think it is much more efficient on the whole than voluntary breath control is. You can deliberately force your mind through channels of deductions and associations in search of a solution to some problem and before long you have dug mental furrows for yourself and find yourself circling round and round the same limited pathways. If those pathways yield no solution, no amount of further conscious thought will help.

On the other hand, if you let go, then the thinking process comes under automatic involuntary control and is more apt to take new pathways and make erratic associations you would not think of consciously. The solution will then come while you *think* you are not *thinking*. . . .

How often does this "Eureka phenomenon" happen? How often is there a flash of deep insight during a moment of relaxation, this triumphant cry of "I've got it! I've got it!" which must surely be a moment of the purest ecstasy this sorry world can afford?

I wish there were some way we could tell. I suspect that in the history of science it happens *often*; I suspect that very few significant discoveries are made by the pure technique of voluntary thought; I suspect that voluntary thought may possibly prepare the ground (if even that), but that the final touch, the real inspiration, comes when thinking is under involuntary control."

Exercise #3

Do you agree with Asimov's premise that ". . . very few significant discoveries are made by the pure technique of voluntary thought . . .that voluntary thought may possibly prepare the ground (if even that), but that the final touch, the real inspiration, comes when thinking is under involuntary control"? Why?

What do you think Asimov means by the term *inspiration* here? Why do you think he feels that *inspiration* cannot be controlled and forced by voluntary thought? Why do you think he feels that voluntary thought lays the groundwork for the *real inspiration* at the heart of discovery? What do you think he means by the term *discovery* here? Do you think he is limiting *discovery* only to science, or do you feel he has a broader application of the term in mind, too? Why do you think so?

Free Writing #2

Write about a time in your life when you felt a feeling of inspiration that led you to a discovery or insight. Was your experience of inspiration similar to what Asimov describes? How did you know that you were inspired? What did you discover as a result?

Return to the opening pages of "Chapter Five: Investigating" in your textbook, and you will find a series of scenarios that involve the ability to formulate both deductions and inferences. The employee at the self-serve gas station has been instructed to gather and assess data; that process will involve an ability to interpret the data accumulated. Generally, data are interpreted on the basis of what types of logical conclusions can be drawn from the evidence presented. Drawing logical conclusions from data is one of the most important aspects of good investigative writing.

Your college instructors in all your classes want to know not only what information you have found, but what you think of that information. Obviously, this is a two-part process of assessment on an instructor's part, since s/he will be concerned with the quality of the data you have discovered and the soundness of your reasoning as you evaluate, question, and analyze your data. Your ability to draw sound inferences from material you have read and from information you have gathered from other means, like questionnaires and statistical analyses, are at the heart of good investigative writing. They are also at the heart of critical thinking, which encompasses your ability to draw logical conclusions and to defend a thesis, or main idea, that you define from your inferences.

An inference is a conclusion based on available information. Some inferences involve drawing logical conclusions from premises, or moving from the general to the specific (deductive reasoning). You have probably seen this type of reasoning presented to you in terms of a syllogism, or a form of deductive reasoning that involves a major premise, a minor premise, and a conclusion. An example of a syllogism would be: All men are mortal (major premise); Mr. Kazmarzyk is a man (minor premise); therefore, Mr. Kazmarzyk is mortal (conclusion). This conclusion is logically valid and sound based upon the premises from which it has been drawn.

Remember, though, that there is a difference between *logically* valid and experientially *true*. This syllogism happens to be both valid and true, since all men are mortal is a major premise that our experience of the world confirms is true. But the syllogism, All men have three ears; Alvin Clark is a man; therefore, Alvin Clark has three ears, is logically valid but not experientially true. In most of the inferences and reasoning judgments we make, we are much more concerned with conclusions that are valid and experientially true than we are with conclusions that are valid logically but "untrue" in that they bear no resemblance to our experience of the world.

Assumption number one in writing investigative papers is that the more information you have the better the inferences you can draw from your data. If I see you run into one of your classes after the bell has rung, I can conclude that you are late to class, but I cannot accurately deduce the reason why. I can posit some guesses--like possibly you overslept, or maybe you met a friend on the way to class, got talking, and lost sight of the time--but I have no way of knowing if these conclusions are correct until I gather more information. As I gather more information, some guesses or assumptions will prove more plausible than others, and some will be eliminated as implausible. By this process I will reason my way to more sound conclusions until I have the one that most accurately explains the information at hand.

Group Exercise #2

Let the class determine what types of conclusions can be drawn from the following data. Which of the conclusions seem more logical and sound, which do not? Why might that be?

1. Fifty-seven robberies of convenience stores occur in Townesville, U.S.A. The police investigate, locate, and arrest the criminals involved. As the police compile their data for their crime reports, they discover that 36% of those arrested for the convenience store robberies were high on marijuana at the time, 11% were high school dropouts, and 63% were wearing red shirts at the time of the robbery.

Cityview has one of the highest crime rates in America. When a survey is conducted, it is discovered that the Cityview municipal water supply is one of the three most polluted water supply systems in America. It is also discovered that Cityview residents buy 14.5% more toy machine guns, space weapon systems, and laser beam rockets as gifts for their children than residents of other cities in America with equivalent populations.

During the 1960's and 1970's, the divorce rate in America nearly doubled. The 1960's and 1970's were also the era in which the greatest gains were made for the Civil Rights movement and for the Women's Liberation movement.

A good source for investigative writing is the assignments you receive from your teachers. Interestingly enough, often your assignments represent problem-solving activities in themselves for you to decipher. Very few of the assignments you receive in college will emphasize the amassing of information alone. Very few, if any, will ask you to give back information without in some way interpreting or responding to the issues associated with that information. In essence, many assignments seek to indicate to you that "truth" has multiple perspectives and that often the idea of right vs. wrong becomes a much more complicated matter than an either/or decision or determination. Thus, your assignments become opportunities for examining different perspectives upon an issue.

Often assignments emphasize that *how* one solves a problem is as important as the solution itself. Since writing is a way of revealing a student's thought processes, both to the student and the teacher, many teachers assign research topics that require students to investigate a particular issue and relate it to contemporary society. If you were given this assignment, it is important to note that you are being asked to: (1) identify an issue (which may also be a matter of definition, since what is an "issue" to one person may not be to another); (2) investigate that issue's ramifications; and (3) relate that issue to contemporary society, which is another way of saying see relationships between or draw inferences about X and Y.

This is a complex task, and failure to execute it well at any stage of the process can lead to a weak paper. If you don't clearly define your issue or show its relevance, then most of the assignment will not work. If you do not investigate your issue fully, it will also be impossible for you to make a convincing case for the relationship between your issue (X) and contemporary society (Y). So, the first investigative task to undertake with any assignment you are given by your teachers involves figuring out what you are being asked to do in the assignment.

Group Exercise #3

Let the class determine what critical thinking skills are involved with each of the assignments from an art history class that follow. In other words, what is the student being asked to do in the assignment to complete the assignment successfully?

1. Francois Boucher's painting *Mercury Confiding the Infant Bacchus to the Nymphs of Nysa* (1769) presents a mythological subject. Using this painting as a point of departure, discuss the relationship between *myth* and *religion*, and discuss whether or not this work is a religious work of art. The painting should be analyzed formally, its subject explained, and put into its historical context. Feel free to refer to other works of art to support and amplify your comments.

[A subsidiary issue of importance: What do you feel is meant by the phrase, "Using this painting as a point of departure . . ."?]

2. Compare and contrast Claude Lorrain's *Coast Scene with Europa and the Bull* (1634) and Edvard Munch's *Three Girls on a Bridge* (c. 1904-07). Analyze formal similarities and dissimilarities between the compositions, and, placing the works into their historical contexts, discuss the values that they seem to express.

[Subsidiary issue of interest: What is meant by the phrase, "placing the works into their historical contexts"?

3. However different the *Standing Shaka Buddha* (c. 1210) and Piet Mondrian's *Composition No. 7 (Facade)* (1914) appear, they both intend the viewer to enter a state of contemplation. Discuss how the works go about this formally and the success to which they achieve this goal.

91

As you investigate the assignments you are given to write about, notice first the directional verbs that you are given, like *discuss, compare and contrast, define, analyze, relate, describe, consider, investigate.* Each of these verbs will indicate to you the direction you should pursue with your assignment. Consider, for example, the concepts represented by the following directional verbs:

Analyze
Separate into parts and discuss, examine, or interpret each part.

Compare
Examine two or more things and show similarities.

Contrast
Examine two or more things and show differences.

Criticize
Analyze and make reasoned judgments about.

Define
Give the meaning of a term or concept.

Describe
Give a detailed account. Indicate characteristics and qualities.

Discuss
Weigh out the pros and cons of an issue.

Enumerate
Make a list of ideas, aspects, parts, etc.

Evaluate
Give a reasoned opinion about (especially in terms of the merit of a particular work or idea).

Explain
Describe how something functions. Give a meaning or definition for.

Identify
Indicate what a thing is or what it is composed of. Similar to describe.

Illustrate
Give examples about. Describe.

Interpret
Comment upon. Explain the meaning of.

Outline
Give an historical overview. Describe main ideas or parts.

Prove
Support with facts.

State
Explain clearly and succinctly.

Summarize
Give the main points or highlights. Give a condensed account.

Trace
Give an historical overview [outline]. Show a chronological or sequential order of events.

[Adapted from David B. Ellis, *Becoming a Master Student*]

Understanding the significance of these directional verbs can help immensely with your writing, especially in the taking of essay exams, in which these words often indicate the type of reasoning and cognitive skills a professor is expecting. Being aware of directional verbs can really assist you in organizing your material in such a way that it reveals a clear line of reasoning consistent with the intellectual exercise and the information the professor wished to derive from the assignment.

Now apply your new-found knowledge about directional verbs and the structure of responding to assignments to an analysis of an essay. The following paper was written by a student in a religion class to address the topic of theodicy, or the issue of God's justice. The paper represents an investigative assignment in that the student was to read a series of articles on the topic and then respond with an overview and a definition of his own. Specifically, the assignment directed the student in this fashion: "Write an essay in which you state and provide a rationale for your views on the problem of theodicy, comparing and contrasting your perspectives with those of the Biblical material we have studied. Include discussions of the issues of innocent suffering, the theory of retribution, the motivations for ethical behavior, and the bases for finding meaning in life. 3-5 pages."

Now, let's look at the assignment and determine what is being called for in this investigative piece. First, obviously, the student is being told to write an essay, so there is an inherent assumption that this piece will reflect an essay form of a clear opening, a well-stated and well-reasoned thesis, a development of the thesis through clear reasoning and supportive examples, and a conclusion that leads to an assessment of the essay's largest insight and that brings all elements of the essay, as a whole, into perspective.

Second, the student is being told to "state and provide a rationale" for his views, which is another way of saying "present a reasoned argument for your perspective." A rationale suggests the fundamental reasons for something, or the logical basis, as well as an exposition of the principles or reasons for one's beliefs. This is the *core* of what the student is being asked to do. If the essay is not logical and well-reasoned, it will not be judged to be an essay of high quality and will receive a low grade.

Third, the student is being asked to deal with some very specific issues and to include them in the discussion. The teacher wants the student to compare and contrast his views with those of the Biblical material (the assigned readings) the class has studied. In addition, the student is to discuss the issues of innocent suffering, the theory of retribution, the motivations for ethical behavior, and the bases for finding meaning in life.

To understand how the student might begin his essay, let's reformulate these requirements of the assignment into a different order and understanding. First, this assignment is to be a response to the issue of God's justice, written in an essay fashion that involves a clear statement of a thesis. Second, the essay is to take the form of a rationale, or well-reasoned argument. The student can safely assume that the issue is *not* the perspective adopted but the manner in which one defends that perspective through clear reasoning. Third, the essay's argument is to focus upon a comparison and contrast of the student's views with the Biblical material assigned and to include four issues the teacher has stressed.

In short, the student has been asked to reveal, through a well-reasoned argument, his understanding of the issue of God's justice by comparing his views with Biblical statements and by including in his discussion the four concepts of innocent suffering, retribution, motivations for ethical behavior, and the bases for finding meaning in life. Failure to execute effectively any of these requirements of the assignment will result in a lower grade for the student. To this extent, this assignment can be viewed as any experience in problem solving. Here are the requirements (or the design) of the problem, and now the task is to solve the problem by responding to its concerns. If you are asked to perform a swan dive, there are certain requirements of the execution that give shape, design, form to he swan dive and distinguish it from other types of dives. If you are asked to build a chair from a block of wood, there are certain requirements of the form that indicate what you should do to accomplish your goal. The idea of the chair in your mind will shape the chair that you design and give form to in actuality. This same principle is at work in the making of this essay on theodicy. The student is being asked to provide a rationale about a subject and to address a set of sub-topics related to that subject. Like the swan dive, or the chair, a rationale has a certain shape or design (requirements of form) that give it its definition and meaning. If the student is successful, his essay will reveal the design (reflect the form) of a clear, well-reasoned, logical argument on he topic of theodicy.

Now, here's the student's essay. For **Exercise #4,** determine how well you think the student has fulfilled the terms of this investigative assignment.

"The Issue of God's Justice"

There are different views on the problem of God's justice. One person can have different beliefs from another. It all depends on a person's faith in what he believes. This faith will lead him in his life. My faith in God and Jesus leads me to believe that it is not God that is unjust but that society on earth is unjust. There is suffering on earth and there is injustice which provide motivation for my ethical behavior and for a meaning in life.

Suffering is seen everywhere in the world. There are many kinds of suffering with no solutions to any of them. I believe that suffering is a part of life. An entire nation can suffer in a war, or an individual can suffer, like the many hungry in the United States today. It must be clarified that suffering today and suffering in the Bible are different. Today, we do not have the problem of another nation ruling and exiling us, but there are still other types of suffering. Jesus had said that his followers will suffer and die just like he suffered and died. Even before Jesus, there was innocent suffering caused by such countries as Assyria and Babylonia who took the Israelites into exile. During their exile, the Israelites questioned God's justice. They did not feel that they deserved the exile since it was their ancestors that did not listen to God. They were following God's word but were still suffering. I believe there is a point to all this suffering. Suffering has always been around and will always be around. It is a result from society and the contradictions within it. Contradictions come from conflicts between earthly beings which cannot be resolved by anyone, not even God.

All this suffering begs the question of whether there is any justice from God. My belief is that there is justice but not on Earth. There is, or course, justice made by man which everyone is familiar with, which sometimes does fail to punish the guilty. There is the other type of justice which is decided after the Resurrection. Through Jesus I believe in the Resurrection that the proper rewards or punishments will be given to individuals after death. In Second Isaiah, the Suffering Servant said that the weakest will be protected. But then in the Apocalyptic Literature, we do not see the weakest protected, but martyred while the bad were in power. This shows that there is no real justice on Earth. Then Jesus said to "Love your neighbor" in order to have peace on Earth, furthermore, have faith in God. Through this faith and right doing, you will be resurrected after death and given justice. The injustice on earth is what results in suffering; both go together stemming from each other. They are man-made in a society that has many problems which no one can solve. So, real justice is with God after the Resurrection.

This suffering and injustice are what become the source for my ethical behavior. Since I believe in the Resurrection, then I have to do good on Earth to be accepted in the Kingdom of God. I realize that if I do good then I have a chance at a better life on Earth and also with God. But if I do bad, then society with its man-made laws will punish me and so will God after my death. In Deuteronomy, the thought was that God is just, we are wicked, and we should repent. This is somewhat true in that God is just, our society is wicked, and we should follow the ethical laws to receive God's justice.

This suffering and injustice present a dim view for finding meaning in life. But it seems logical that if you live an ethical life then God will reward you. This is the basis for finding meaning in life--to do your best on earth in order to enter the Kingdom of God. THis was a theme throughout the Old and New Testament, to do good on earth to be rewarded by God, except that no one knew how and when they would be given justice until Jesus defined it. Ecclesiastes, on the other hand, had a varying theme. This prophet found material pleasure on earth because he felt he could not count on God for everything. This also is seen today, which makes things a bit complex. People today, and I do as well, find pleasure in materialistic objects and live to be successful in life. But Jesus said to give up your riches, humbling yourself to others. But I think that this kind of thought Jesus intended for society then and needs to be adapted o today's society. If a person is ethical and good in his own society, then God will judge him in comparison to others in his society.

Just to clarify my beliefs, I will illustrate them in my life. There is suffering all around me. War brings suffering to people in the world every day, and I suffer like everyone in my society just having to deal with daily life. This really is not dramatic suffering, but just everyday problems that can still be called suffering. I also see around me much injustice with the homeless and the hungry. There are many cases where the law is unjust to the innocent by letting criminals free because of minor technical details. An example of this is a criminal who was set free because his rights were not read to him. So we see the innocent people becoming victims. The basis of my ethical behavior is to live a happy life without becoming a victim of the bad side of society. I know that if I strive for the good, then I have a chance at reaching it. Entering the Kingdom of God is not a concrete goal that I always think about, but it adds meaning to my life whenever I feel down.

Exercise #4

As a continuation of your directions for Exercise #4, evaluate the student's essay on "The Issue of God's Justice." What grade of A, B, C, D, or F would you give to this essay? Defend your choice of grade by spelling out and defining specific criteria for grading and evaluation.

Do you feel this essay fulfills the requirements of the assignment? Why or why not?

Do you feel this essay is a good essay or a weak essay that reveals a large number of problems? What might those problems be?

If you had to counsel this student on how he could improve this essay through revision and rewriting, what advice would you give to the student? What areas do you feel would need the most work in the revision?

Have you learned anything from looking at this essay and assessing its structure and overall effect that you could apply to your own writing? What do you feel you have learned?

Group Exercise #4

Let the class divide into groups of four or five and consider the essay, "The Issue of God's Justice." Each group is to outline and discuss what it feels to be the organizational pattern of the essay. Around what principles of thought and argumentation are the sections (or paragraphs) of the essay structured? What transitions indicate changes in thought in the essay? Are they effective? Does this essay's structure indicate that it is clearly developed and well-reasoned or digressive and poorly connected in terms of logic? Why might that be?

Perhaps in your individual or group assessment of "The Issue of God's Justice" you noticed the lack of clear and convincing examples in the essay. An example is a specific instance that is used to support or explain a more general statement. By adding concreteness to a statement, examples can be very effective and persuasive. Weaker essays tend to stay at a very high level of generality and fail to use examples as a focus for their ideas and as a means for adding interest and variety to their topic.

The use of examples in investigative writing is particularly important, since effective examples can persuade readers that what is being said is accurate and worth listening to. Examples not only are succinct and efficient in that one example can take the place of pages of general discussion, but examples can give writing the edge it needs to be convincing. In investigative writing, examples drawn from personal experience can be especially convincing because they present the writer as having direct knowledge of the subject, and this can be more convincing to a a reader than a third-person account. Of course, not all subjects will lend themselves to the use of personal examples, but, in instances in which this is possible, the immediacy of the first-hand example can be very convincing.

Part of this reasoning is at work in the use of questionnaires. If the writer has designed the questionnaire and conducted the survey, there is an immediacy to the conclusions drawn that contributes to the effectiveness of the writing as a whole. Statistics drawn from other sources and used by the writer can be very convincing, too, but not in a first-hand, personal manner but more along the line of the objective presentation of data. In structuring your investigative writing, it is important to consider the effects you want to achieve with your reader and how your goals will influence the approach taken to your investigative essay.

In investigative writing, the use of examples also helps keep your thesis in focus by commenting upon, expanding, and supporting it. Examples also give readers the information they need to understand the material you are presenting. This factor is extremely important in investigative writing if the topic of your investigation is a highly complex or abstract issue. Examples well-used clarify; they also add more interest and intrigue by enlivening large general statements and making them come alive for your reader. Without examples, your essay would contain one general, abstract discussion after another that would offer little appeal to your reader's imagination and intellect.

For examples to be effective, they must be relevant, sufficient in number, and representative. A clear connection must exist between your examples and your thesis; one telling example or several clear examples that enhance your point will help defend your views; and your examples should represent the full range of the class of items you are discussing. If, for example, you are investigating the influence of television upon religious ministries, you would not want to confine yourself to only one religious denomination, or to only churches in urban areas. You would want to investigate and include a range of examples from a number of religious denominations and from both rural and urban areas as well. Similarly, you would want to keep your examples relevant to your thesis, so going off the track to discuss the influence of television upon contemporary society as a whole would be an unnecessary tangent that would confuse, if not distract and bore, your audience.

Exercise #5

Write an investigative essay in which you discuss the relative merits of reading versus television. Use a number of examples from your own experience to illustrate your points, as well as information drawn from a questionnaire you design to find out information about people's reading and television viewing habits and preferences.

Exercise #6

Write an investigative essay in which you illustrate how a family dinner or a neighborhood social gathering is indicative of the values and social attitudes of the group that attended. Use examples to support your views and also indicate the investigative approach and line of deductive or inductive reasoning you followed in your essay. Are there ways, too, that you could connect your investigative research to other sources of information such as articles, books, interviews, surveys, or questionnaires? Borrowing a line from your textbook, "If you had more time to work on this essay, which sources would you investigate further?"

Point/Counterpoint: Considering Opposing Arguments

1. What is your sense of the value of investigative writing? How do you differentiate investigative writing from other kinds of writing, like description, narration, process analysis, etc., that are also designed to convey information to a reader?

2. "Investigative writing begins with questions to uncover truths not generally known or accepted." Do you agree? Why or why not?

3. Professor Southworth, in discussing investigative writing with her composition class, states, "The *ideal* of investigative writing is that all investigations be thorough and as unbiased as humanly possible. The *reality*, unfortunately, is very much different in that most investigative pieces are not very thorough and only give as much background material as is necessary to get the piece going and, as for bias on the part of the investigator, that's a built-in assumption in all investigative pieces. The truth is class, that the investigator slants the approach and the findings in the directions that he or she chooses and reports the results that support these views while minimizing or overlooking results that would support the opposing views."
Do you agree with Professor Southworth's views? Why or why not?

4. Writing a profile of an individual is an important aspect of investigative writing. To indicate how approach and slant can influence investigative writing, choose a public figure from the present or the past and write about his or her life as if (1) you were a supporter trying to get other people to see this person in a positive light and (2) you were a detractor trying to get others to see this person for the scoundrel he or she really is.
In both essays, use the exact same set of facts and details about the person's life but vary your interpretation of this data. What does an exercise of this sort indicate to you about slant, perspective, and bias in investigative writing?

5. Return to the essay, "The Triumph of the Wheel," by Lewis Grossberger in your text. Briefly summarize the main points Grossberger is trying to make about the game show, "The Wheel of Fortune." Conduct a survey of your own amongst your friends or classmates to see if they agree with Grossberger's conclusions. If they disagree, suggest reasons for this difference. If they agree with Grossberger, what additional conclusions can you draw from this information about the reasons for the popularity of this TV game show?
Do you think the reasons for this popularity are limited exclusively to "Wheel of Fortune" or would they apply equally as well to other popular TV shows. Conduct an investigation to see if your views are correct and write up the results of your inquiry.

6. Return to your textbook and re-read the section on "Shaping" that discusses the "inverted pyramid" style of organization for an essay, as well as chronological order, definition, and comparison contrast as means for structuring an investigative piece. Do you agree with these methods? How would you evaluate their effectiveness? Do you think they contribute a great deal to an essay's structure, or do you feel they are formulaic devices that make essays seem very much alike and highly predictable in pattern?

Are there alternative methods of organization you would propose for investigative essays? What would those methods be and how would they differ from the ones proposed by your textbook?

7. How would you structure an investigative writing to support or negate the conclusions contained in the following excerpt from Marya Mannes' "Television: The Splitting Image" that appeared in the November 1970 issue of *The Saturday Review of Literature*?

Besides, aren't commercials in the public interest? Don't they help you choose what to buy? Don't they provide needed breaks from programming? Aren't many of them brilliantly done, and some of them funny? And now, with the new sexual freedom, all those gorgeous chicks with their shining hair and gleaming smiles? And if you didn't have commercials taking up a good part of each hour, how on earth would you find enough program material to fill the endless space/time void?

8. How would you design or structure an investigative essay about the issues raised by Anne Morrow Lindbergh in this excerpt from *Gift from the Sea*?

With a new awareness, both painful and humorous, I begin to understand why the saints were rarely married women. I am convinced it has nothing inherently to do, as I once supposed, with chastity or children. It has to do primarily with distractions. The bearing, rearing, feeding and educating of children; the running of a house with its thousand details; human relationships with their myriad pulls-- woman's normal occupations in general run counter to creative life, or contemplative life, or saintly life. The problem is not merely one of *Woman and Career*, *Woman and the Home*, *Woman and Independence*. It is more basically: how to remain whole in the midst of the distractions of life; how to remain balanced, no matter what centrifugal forces tend to pull one off center; how to remain strong, no matter what shocks come in at the periphery and tend to crack the hub of the wheel.

What issues of human life and of family life is Lindbergh raising? By what investigative methods could you assess the validity of the concerns she is addressing? Do you think these concerns apply to women, in general, or only to Lindbergh's life? How would you investigate the universality and relevance of her concerns? How would you structure and present your finds to your audience?

9. Design and write an investigative essay on your experience of the popular media. You are asked to explore some aspect of television, film, video, radio, or newspapers and magazines. What conclusions about contemporary society did your investigative study of the popular media lead you to discover?

10. Study your local newspaper for at least one week, paying particular attention to the front page headlines and accompanying story. Based upon your investigation, what logically and reasonably could you say were the major concerns or issues facing society today? Do you feel that such conclusions can be drawn from a study of newspaper headlines, or do you feel that news and public issues change so quickly and respond so dramatically to unpredictable world events that no reasonable and predictive conclusions can be drawn?

11. Of the methods of investigative writing presented to you by your textbook and your workbook, which one would seem (or has proven) to be the most helpful to you? Which one the least helpful? Why might this be, in both instances?

12. Are there future instances or situations in which you can foresee writing investigative pieces? What might those situations be? If you cannot perceive yourself ever doing any type of investigative writing, do you feel your study of the methods and requirements of investigative writing has been a waste of your time? Why or why not?

SUMMARY AND ASSESSMENT PAGE

What ideas from *CHAPTER FIVE: INVESTIGATING* (in either your textbook or your workbook) helped you the most with your writing? What ideas or techniques did you hope to get from this chapter but did not? What steps do you intend to take to learn those ideas or techniques?

"WRITING, LIKE LIFE ITSELF, IS A VOYAGE OF DISCOVERY"

--HENRY MILLER

CHAPTER SIX: EXPLAINING

An explanation makes something comprehensible by removing any obscurity surrounding the object's or event's definition or experience. In other instances, an explanation enables us to give logical causes or reasons for an object's or event's existence and implications.

Of all the modes of discourse, explanation is the one we most commonly use in our everyday experience of the world. Like most rhetorical modes, though, explanation seldom occurs independently of other modes of thought. When we explain, we also describe, define, observe, remember, perhaps even compare and contrast, analyze, investigate, argue, and explore.

Exercise #1

Your textbook defines the process of explanation in this fashion: "Explaining goes beyond investigating the facts and reporting information; it analyzes a subject into its component parts and then shows how the parts fit into some pattern of relationships. Its goal is to clarify--for a particular group of readers-- *what* something is, *how* it happened or should happen, or *why* it exists or occurs."

Do you agree with this definition/explanation of *explaining*? If so, how would you use it (apply it) to explain the process of explaining?

Explanatory writing often depends a great deal on written materials as the basis of essays. To explain a process or the reason for a particular event often requires a good deal of research. This distinguishing factor is an important one. In previous chapters and writing exercises, you used both observation and recollection as the basis for your writings. Now the focus shifts, and you will move into the type of writing that is more characteristic of most of your academic courses and certainly of the business and professional world.

This change to a different source of materials for your writing should not be frightening or disturbing. You will not be abandoning skills you have learned, only adding to your repertoire of abilities. The two predominant skills to learn will be the ability to restate a written passage, or *paraphrasing*, and the ability to abstract the main idea from a passage, or *summarizing*.

Students often mistake these two key skills, thinking that a paraphrase is a summary, or that a summary is a paraphrase. In a similar fashion, students often think that a summary includes every idea, every word, when, actually, a summary or abstract *reduces* the size of the original material. If this is not the case in your summary, you have only restated or rewritten the passage, not summarized it.

The purpose of a paraphrase is to convert a difficult and complex passage to a more simple statement of the idea. A paraphrase works on simplifying and clarifying a passage and functions like a type of intellectual translation from one mode of expression to another.

A summary, on the other hand, shortens a passage to its essential elements by rephrasing the key ideas and eliminating illustrations, explanations, and non-essential exposition of details. A summary is sometimes also called an *abstract* or a *precis*.

The first step in both paraphrasing and summarizing is to identify key words and establish their meaning. All sentences have words that are more important than others and are more laden with meaning. Identifying these key words is the beginning of an effective summary or paraphrase. The second step is to mark out all words or phrases that are not essential, and the third step is to look up in a dictionary all words you do not know.

When you have a clear idea in your mind of what the passage is communicating, the final step is to write your idea of the passage's content in a clear and simplified sentence or paragraph. The length of your paraphrase, summary, abstract, or precis will depend upon the task you have been assigned. Some paraphrases and summaries are one sentence long; others are one paragraph long. Sometimes a word-length designation is given, like "Summarize the following passage in one hundred words or fewer." In all summaries and paraphrases, the length of what you do and the approach you take will be determined by the assignment or directions you have been given, or by the requirements of the particular piece you are writing.

Often when you tell how to do something or explain how something works, you are presenting a process. A process pays special attention to sequence, in that events in a process occur in a sequence and usually as a result or interaction of one step with another. Generally, we tend to think of instructions and process explanations as the same thing, but actually there are some important differences. Instructions enable a person to *perform* the process. A process explanation, however, helps a person to *understand* the process. The purpose of both events, giving instructions and describing processes, is, however, to inform; and, thus, each is still a branch of explanation.

Many of your college classes and your professional work settings will call for process explanations. Your biology teacher may ask you to explain the process of cell division, or your business teacher may ask you to generate a flow chart and explain the sequence of information transfer within a particular business or organization. If you design an exceptional program of patient care for your social work class, you might even be called upon to write a set of instructions telling others how to duplicate the process. In business and professional settings, there might be no end to the type of explanations of process you might be called upon to provide, particularly if your job involves the training of new personnel.

Exercise #2

Write a short essay explaining your writing process. Then use your explanation as a base from which to derive a set of guidelines or directions for instructing others on good procedures to follow in learning how to write.

Expository writing, or writing that explains and informs, is often presented in the form of a proposal that identifies a problem, offers a solution, and attempts to convince the reader to accept the proposed solution. Usually the problem is discussed in some detail, giving background information about its causes and history. The solutions that are proposed to address the problem are outlined in detail, together with ways the solutions can be implemented. In extended proposals, some authors even anticipate opposing viewpoints or doubts that might arise about the proposed solutions. In essence, proposals represent a unique type of explanatory writing in that they can involve definition, description, investigation, cause and effect analysis, argumentation, and problem-solving analysis.

Proposals can be written for an informed audience, aware of a problem and seeking solutions to it, or to an uninformed audience who must first be made aware of the fact that a problem exists. Both types of proposals, though, involve the ability to analyze a problem and persuade a reader to accept particular solutions. The best of proposals not only present solutions but also anticipate objections to the solutions proposed and counter those objections with clear reasoning.

While you might not be asked specifically to write a proposal in your college courses, it is important to remember that proposal writing involves another skill that you will be called upon to use often--and that is the ability to formulate a position (or line of reasoning) and to defend your views. Since one of the most common complaints from teachers in all disciplines is that students do not know how to make an argument, learning how to define a problem and propose solutions for its elimination seems a worthy goal.

When teachers indicate that students do not know how to make an argument, they generally do not mean that students do not know how to take an opposing position. Rather, they mean that students have difficulty defending a position in any systematic way. Finding good reasons for a position and presenting those reasons in an ordered fashion seem to be very difficult for most college students. Even the two most common modes of reasoning, *deduction*, in which the argument moves from a general statement to a particular instance, and *induction*, in which the argument moves from particular instances to a general truth, seem too complicated, or perhaps only elusive, for most students who would rather present their ideas in the random and often haphazard fashion that their ideas originally appear to them in their minds. While the flow of your ideas is a good place to *start* your argument from (like a free writing, a brainstorming session, or a journal entry), arguments must progress from a flow of ideas toward a structure that lays out the implications of the argument and the best ways for the reader to respond to the issues involved.

Often an important factor in writing a good proposal or formulating a good argument is the clear establishment of your *ethos*. *Ethos is a Greek rhetorical term for the character of the* speaker or writer in an argument--the "voice" behind the logic of the words. Winifred Bryan Horner in *Rhetoric in the Classical Tradition* defines *ethos* as "the ethical argument of a discourse that depends on establishing the credibility and goodwill of the speaker." In the *Rhetoric*, Aristotle considered *ethos*, or the character of the speaker or writer, to be the most effective kind of persuasion, stating:

Persuasion is achieved by the speaker's personal character when the speech is so spoken as to make us think him credible. We believe good men more fully and more readily than others; this is true generally whatever the question is, and absolutely true where exact certainty is impossible and opinions divided.

Aristotle makes an important point with regard to issues about which there is a great deal of divided opinion and merit to both sides of the argument. In these instances, audiences will respond to the integrity of the speaker/writer and admire and relate to those who speak or write with honesty, integrity, and fair-mindedness on a given topic.

If you doubt the powerful impact the *ethos* or character of the speaker can have upon an audience, take a look at contemporary advertising. Sports figures serve as spokespersons for automobile companies; movie stars push perfumes and colognes. Venerable movie or TV stars who are identified with family virtues in the various roles they play urge audiences to buy a particular brand of frozen foods, while character actors dressed as nurses or doctors extol the virtues of a brand of cold medicine, or toothpaste, or headache remedy. What do these individuals have to do with the products they represent? Very little in terms of true expertise, but a great deal in terms of *ethos*. When an actor who has been on TV for years as a father figure and symbol of paternal wisdom pushes a particular brand of automobile, we believe him. The fact that he may know little about the automobile's design or quality is overshadowed in our minds by our sense of his character as he speaks, informs, and persuades us to purchase the automobile he is endorsing.

Exercise #3

For this exercise, take one of the papers you have written recently for a college or high school class and examine the *ethos* you have established in your paper. What methods have you used to establish your credibility as a writer/speaker? How effective are the methods you have chosen in terms of their effect upon an audience? If you were given the chance to rewrite this paper, would you maintain the same *ethos* or try to establish another sense of your character and credibility in the paper? Why or why not?

In Aristotle's view, the credibility of a speaker is established through intelligence, virtue, and goodwill. Intelligence is demonstrated through the speaker's personal knowledge of the subject and through well-reasoned arguments that are balanced and fair, while virtue and goodwill are shown through the speaker's ability to identify with the values and interests of the audience. In examining the *ethos* you have chosen to establish in your paper, have you revealed intelligence, virtue, and goodwill? Why or why not?

Exercise #4

To give you practice with defining a sense of your *ethos*, write an essay in which you discuss yourself today--your current life, your situation, and your attitudes--and an essay in which you discuss yourself tomorrow--your hopes, dreams, plans, and goals. Focus upon your *ethos* in both essays. What did writing these two essays tell you about yourself and about your *ethos* in relation to your writing?

Exercise #5

In the following excerpt from "Listen! The Wind" by Anne Morrow Lindbergh, describe the *ethos* that Lindbergh establishes in this essay. In what ways does she accomplish this end? What does Lindbergh's essay reveal of the relationship between *ethos* and one's ability to explain in an essay?

This little cockpit of mine became extraordinarily pleasing to me, as much so as a furnished study at home. Every corner, every crack, had significance. Every object meant something. Not only the tools I was working with, the transmitter and receiver, the key and the antenna reel; but even the small irrelevant objects on the side of the fuselage, the little black hooded light, its face now turned away from me, the shining arm and knob of the second throttle, the bright switches and handles, the colored wires and copper pipes: all gave me, in a strange sense, as much pleasure as my familiar books and pictures might at home. The pleasure was perhaps not esthetic but came from a sense of familiarity, security, and possession. I invested them with an emotional significance of their own, since they had been through so much with me. They made up this comfortable, familiar, tidy, compact world that was mine . . . . Outside the night rushed by. How nice to be in your own little room, to pull your belongings around you, to draw in like a snail in his shell, to work!

Exercise #6

Lindbergh draws an analogy in her essay between the cockpit and the home. In what ways is this analogy effective in establishing her *ethos* as a speaker? In what ways, if any, is it not effective? Do you feel that her analogy of comparing her cockpit to a home environment weakens or strengthens her claim to credibility on this topic? What effect upon her audience do you think this analogy will have in establishing Lindbergh's *ethos* of intelligence, virtue, and goodwill?

Exercise #7

For Exercise #7, consider the *ethos* that each author presents in the following passages. Write both a description and an explanation of your sense of the *ethos* each author projects in his or her work. What factors lead you to your conclusions and your sense of the author's *ethos*? Do you feel the *ethos established in each of these writings works for or against* the credibility the writer is trying to establish? Do you feel it works for or against a sense of engagement between the writer and the audience in terms of relating to and understanding the piece? Which author's *ethos* seems to you the most engaging or credible? Why? Write an explanation of your choice and include your reasoning for your decision. Finally, do you consider each of these excerpts good examples of explanatory essays? Why or why not?

a). Howard Ensign Evans, "The Story of Fireflies"

The light organs of fireflies are complex structures, and recent studies using the electron microscope show them to be even more complex than one supposed. Each is composed of three layers: an outer "window," simply a transparent portion of the body wall; the light organ proper; and an inner layer of opaque whitish cells filled with granules of uric acid, the so-called "reflector." The light organ proper contains large, slablike light cells, each of them filled with large granules and much smaller, dark granules, the latter tending to be concentrated around the numerous air tubes and nerves penetrating the light organ. These smaller granules were once assumed by some persons to be luminous bacteria, but we now know they are mitochondria, the source of ATP and therefore the energy of light production. The much larger granules that fill most of the light cells are still of unknown function; perhaps they serve as the source of luceriferin.

b). Erma Bombeck, "Se Habla English"

When my son entered the first grade, his teacher asked to see me. She began our meeting by telling me, "He verbalizes during class,periodically engages in excursions up and down the aisle, has no viable goals and seemingly no definitive conception of his role expectations. Peer pressure seems advised at this time."
"Are you trying to tell me my son is goofing off?"
"I would not have expressed it in the vernacular, but you are correct."

c). Natalie Goldberg, *Writing Down the Bones*: *Freeing the Writer Within*

Writers live twice. They go along with their regular life, are as fast as anyone in the grocery store, crossing the street, getting dressed for work in the morning. But there's another part of them that they have been training. The one that lives everything a second time. That sits down and sees their life again and goes over it. Looks at the texture and details.

In a rainstorm, everyone quickly runs down the street with umbrellas, raincoats, newspapers over their heads. Writers go back outside in the rain with a notebook in front of them and a pen in hand. They look at the puddles, watch them fill, watch the rain splash in them. You can say a writer practices being dumb. Only a dummy would stand out in the rain and watch a puddle. If you're smart, you get in out of the rain so you won't catch cold, and you have health insurance, in case you get sick. If you're dumb, you are more interested in the puddle than in your security and insurance or in getting to work on time.

d). Elizabeth Bruss, *Beautiful Theories*

It was late in the 1960s when the symptoms, heretofore fugitive and for the most part manageable, could no longer be ignored. The Anglo-American literary community, which had been erected on the rock of Johnsonian empiricism and Arnoldian sensibility, found itself suddenly possessed by an alien spirit of speculation, infected by an unspeakable cant of theoretical abstractions. The signs were everywhere (as, indeed, everything seemed destined to become yet another sign): Professional meetings that might once have spent their sessions in admiring the visionary system of a Blake or a Yeats turned instead to the great system-building critics and the deconstructive subverters of those systems; graduate programs in "poetics" began to displace the more familiar period specializations; and the annual bibliography of the Modern Language Association (which had made no official mention of "literary theory" until 1960, and then continued to group it together, indifferently, with "aesthetics" and "literary criticism" until 1967) was reorganized to create a separate subdivision devoted exclusively to "Literary Criticism and Literary Theory"--and the number of entries immediately began to swell from a scant two hundred in 1967 to over six hundred in 1975. All at once the books that were most honored, most frequently cited or condemned, were no longer scholarly monographs on the roots of Restoration comedy or readings of the later Eliot but were instead the collected papers of the latest international symposium (e.g. *The Languages of Criticism and the Sciences of Man*)-- books in which one set of critics offered introductions to another, complete with histories and arduous appraisals of the structure of their arguments, their ideological positions, even their characteristic rhetorical modes (Culler's *Structuralist Poetics*, Jameson's *Prison-House of Language* and *Marxism and Form*, de Man's *Blindness and Insight*, Said's *Beginnings*, to name but a few key examples).

e). Thomas Hoover, "Zen Culture and the Counter Mind" from *Zen Culture*

The Zen tradition extends back some fifteen hundred years to a wandering Indian teacher of meditation named Bodhidharma. As Indian gurus are fond of doing, Bodhidharma left his homeland and journeyed abroad, following what was in those days a well-beaten trail to China. Upon reaching Nanking, he paused to visit the Chinese Emperor Wu, a man known to be a particularly devout Buddhist. The emperor was delighted to receive his famous Indian guest and proceeded immediately to boast of his own accomplishments. "I have built many temples. I have copied the sacred *sutras*. I have led many to the Buddha. Therefore, I ask you: What is my merit: What reward have I earned? Bodhidharma reportedly growled, "None whatsoever, you Majesty." The emperor was startled but persisted, "Tell me then, what is he most important principle or teaching of Buddhism?" "Vast emptiness," Bodhidharma replied, meaning, of course, the void of nonattachment. Not knowing what to make of his guest, the emperor backed away and inquired, "Who exactly *are* you who stands before me now?" To which Bodhidharma admitted that he had no idea.

Sensing that the emperor was not yet prepared for such teachings, Bodhidharma left the palace and traveled to a mountain monastery to begin a long career of meditation. Over the years his reputation for wisdom gradually attracted many followers--dissident Chinese who rejected classical Buddhism and all its rigmarole in favor of Bodhidharma's meditation, or *dhyana*, a Sanskrit term they pronounced as *Ch'an*-- later to be called Zen by the Japanese. This teaching of meditation and vast emptiness shared very little with other branches of Chinese Buddhism. Ch'an had no sacred images because it had no gods to worship, and it de-emphasized the scriptures, since its central dogma was that dogma was useless. Handed down from master to pupil was the paradoxical teaching that nothing can be taught. According to Ch'an (and Zen), understanding comes only by ignoring the intellect and heeding the instincts, the intuition.

f). Francis Bacon, "Of Studies"

Studies serve for delight, for ornament, and for ability. Their chief use for delight is in privateness, and retiring; for ornament, is in discourse; and for ability, is in the judgment and disposition of business; for expert men can execute, and perhaps judge of the particulars, one by one; but the general counsels, and the plots and marshaling of affairs, come best from those that are learned.

To spend too much time in studies, is sloth; to use them too much for ornament, is affectation; to make judgment wholly by their rules, is the humor of a scholar; they perfect nature and are perfected by experience--for natural abilities are like natural plants, that need pruning by study; and studies themselves do give forth directions too much at large, except they be bounded in by experience. Crafty men condemn studies, simple men admire them, and wise men use them, for they teach not their own use; but that is a wisdom without them, and above them, won by observation.

Read not to contradict and confute, nor to believe and take for granted, nor to find talk and discourse, but to weigh and consider. SOme books are to be tasted, others to be swallowed, and some few to be chewed and digested; that is, some books are to be read only in parts; others to be read, but not curiously; and some few to be read wholly, and with diligence and attention. Some books also may be read by deputy, and extracts made of them by others; but that would be only in the less important arguments, and the meaner sort of books; else distilled books are like common distilled waters, flashy things.

Reading maketh a full man, conference a ready man, and writing an exact man; and, therefore, if a man write little, he had need have a great memory; if he confer little, he had need have a present wit; and if he read little, he had need have much cunning, to seem to know that he doth not. Histories make men wise; poets, witty; the mathematics, subtle; natural philosophy, deep; moral philosophy, grave; logic and rhetoric, able to contend.

Free write for ten or fifteen minutes on the concept of *ethos*. How important do you think *ethos* is to writing? Do you think a concern with *ethos* is an important or an exaggerated concern?

Group Exercise #1

As your textbook indicates, one of the key abilities associated with expository prose, or the art of explaining in writing, is the ability to abstract a central or most important idea (a thesis) from other sources. Applying this principle to the selections included in Exercise #7, have the class divide itself into groups of four or five and work on summarizing the main idea of each of the selections in Exercise #7. Make the abstracts or summaries as brief and succinct as possible; several sentences will do.

After the class has summarized the key idea(s) in each of these selections, have the class discuss the value of summary to writing an explanatory essay. How valuable a skill is the ability to abstract or summarize an idea from a printed source? What is the relationship this skill bears to writing explanatory essays?

One of the techniques your textbook advocates as a patterned strategy for generating ideas for an explanatory essay is a set of questions referred to as "the journalist's questions," which reporters use as a checklist for gathering data: *WHO? WHAT? WHERE? WHEN? WHY? HOW?*

If, for example, your college or university were planning to raise its tuition academic year and you were instructed by your composition teacher to write an explanatory paper that focused on the reasons for this increase, the *WHO? WHAT? WHERE? WHEN? WHY? HOW?* questions might provide a logical structure for the organization of your paper:

WHO? was responsible for the increase? (State government? The Board of Trustees? The President of the university? The educational policies and budget cuts of the federal government?) *WHO?* will be affected by the increase? (All students, or only incoming and transfer students? Will fees for out-of-state students also increase on a proportional basis?)

WHAT? caused the increase? (Lower student enrollments? Higher student enrollments and an increased demand for student services? An expansion in the number of academic programs offered? An increase in administrative costs?) *WHAT?* can be done to avoid the increase? (Will petitions from faculty and students have any effect? Can cuts in sports and recreational programs be proposed as an alternative to a tuition increase? Can students be charged higher fees for courses that require labs rather than all students be charged higher fees across the board?)

WHERE? will the tuition increase be implemented? (In all branches of the state university system, or only at particular universities?) *WHERE?* will students learn of the increase? (Local newspapers? Brochures from the university?)

WHEN? will the tuition increase occur? (Next semester? Next academic year? One year, two years, three years from now?) *WHEN*? will students have the opportunity to voice their opinions about the increase? (The next meeting of the Student Senate? Public forums sponsored by the university at the beginning of each semester?)

WHY? is the increase in tuition being considered? (What will be the long-term benefits of a tuition increase? What are the advantages of solving the university's budget crunch in this fashion rather than with a cut in administrative programs?) *WHY*? were students not informed of the proposed tuition increase earlier in the decision-making process? (Was it an oversight? A deliberate effort to avoid controversy? An insensitivity to students' needs on the part of the administration?)

HOW? will the tuition increase be administered? (Will all students be affected, or only incoming and transfer students? Will students be expected to pay for the tuition increase in one lump sum, or will they be permitted to make installment payments?) *HOW*? will student needs be addressed in response to the increase? (Will there be increased efforts by the administration to secure federal and state educational loans and grants for students? Will the number of work-study jobs on campus be increased?)

The "journalist's questions" provide a rudimentary outline for structuring your paper. They ensure that major issues involved in an assignment are being covered, since you will know what is occurring when, who is responsible, how the process will occur, and what will be some of its consequences. From the "journalist's questions," you can expand your essay to include a more probing analysis of the issues involved and perhaps derive a sense of how your essay should begin and end. A consideration of these questions and the issues they raise can also direct you toward further research and reading about your topic.

Exercise #8

Apply the "journalist's questions" to a problem facing your school or community. How effective were the questions in helping you formulate a structure for your essay? Did the questions enable you to have a sense of what your reader needed to know to understand your essay?

Explanation often involves the use of other rhetorical modes, such as comparison and contrast, process analysis, etc. In each instance of explanation, whatever rhetorical mode you are being called upon to use, be sure you understand the *purpose* involved in the use of the rhetorical mode. For example, if you are being asked for a discussion or explanation of the similarities between two literary texts, consider what is your purpose in the comparison. Are you being asked to explain the texts' merits by comparing their structures and overall quality? Or are you looking at texts from the same historical era to determine and explain cultural and historical influences upon literary texts? The nature of your purpose in the comparison and in the explanation will enable you to know how to proceed. Without a clear sense of purpose, your use of the rhetorical modes may seem digressive and repetitious.

In terms of explanatory essays, comparison and contrast and analogy are two rhetorical modes that can be used quite effectively to make your points more clear. Comparison means to show a likeness, while contrasting shows differences. When you compare or contrast, you show likenesses or differences between two or more persons, objects, or events *for the purpose of making a point*. Never forget this last idea, because many students are content to make the comparison or contrast and let it speak for itself. To be an effective explainer, you must use the comparison or contrast in service of the point you are making, and you must make that point very clear to your audience.

Comparison and contrast can present some complex challenges for writers who use them in explanatory essays. For one, you will need a particularly strong sense of organization and control over your material, for you will have more material to work with. Second, you will need to know two subjects well, rather than the usual one for most essays. If you do not narrow your points well and keep your comparisons and contrasts succinct and insightful, you paper will become digressive and probably flat and uninteresting. Long comparisons and contrasts will seldom be as effective as concise ones for the purposes of an explanatory essay.

A special form of comparison is an *analogy*, which is usually an extended comparison between two things ordinarily thought of as unlike. Analogies are quite good instructional devices, as the Biblical parables and many a minister's sermons indicate, and they are especially fine rhetorical devices for making points clear in an explanation.

When you are faced with complex or specialized terms and ideas to present to a general reading audience, analogies can help make these points clear by giving your readers a mental picture they are more familiar with and can more easily understand. In addition, an analogy is a form of logical inference, since an analogy is based on the assumption that if two things are known to be alike in some ways, they are presumed to be alike in other ways. This factor can often be quite helpful in an explanatory essay designed to be persuasive, as well.

Use an analogy to describe some aspect of your philosophy of life. How does the use of an analogy for explanation influence your sense of self-expression in a free writing?

Exercise #9

Select several works that you feel use analogy effectively as a rhetorical device for explanation and persuasion. In your journal, or for an in-class writing, comment upon the analogies used in these selections and how they contribute to the overall impact and effectiveness of the selections.

As an extension of this assignment, look for the use of analogy in newspaper, magazine, and television advertising. What types of analogies are used most often to make a point and to explain a product's uses and value to an audience? What makes analogies so effective as explanatory and persuasive tools in these advertisements?

Point/Counterpoint: Considering Opposing Arguments

1. Which of the techniques presented to you by your textbook and your workbook for writing explanatory essays seemed to you the most helpful? Which were the least so? Why do you think that might be?

2. In an explanatory essay of your own, explain the value and use of the techniques of branching, observing, remembering, investigating, shaping, defining, classifying, comparing, contrasting, drawing analogies, and analyzing processes to the writing of explanatory essays. If you had to eliminate any *two* techniques from the list above, which two would you eliminate as the least important? Why?

3. Your textbooks states that "explaining and demonstrating relationships is a frequent purpose for writing." Do you agree? Why or why not?

4. Return to your textbook and re-read the selection by psychologist Sukie Colgrave from *Spirit of the Valley: Androgyny and Chinese Thought*. Colgrave states that "the experience of being 'in love' is one of powerful dependency."
Do you agree? Why or why not? How would you explain *dependency* in this context? What do you think Colgrave means by the term? If you had to explain this term through an analogy, what analogy would you choose. Explain the reasons for your choice.

5. Your textbook states that "'Why?' may be the most common question asked by human beings. We are fascinated by the reasons for everything we experience in life."
Do you agree? Why or why not? Explain.

6. Which part of the discussions on explaining presented in either your textbook or your workbook do you think were not explained very well, or at least not as clearly as other sections? In what ways were they unclear? How could they be made more clear? Explain.

SUMMARY AND ASSESSMENT PAGE

What ideas from *CHAPTER SIX: EXPLAINING* (in either your textbook or your workbook) helped you the most with your writing? What ideas or techniques did you hope to get from this chapter but did not? What steps do you intend to take to learn those ideas or techniques?

"IN MOST LIVES INSIGHT HAS BEEN ACCIDENTAL. WE WAIT FOR IT AS PRIMITIVE MAN AWAITED LIGHTENING FOR A FIRE. BUT MAKING MENTAL CONNECTIONS IS OUR MOST CRUCIAL LEARNING TOOL, THE ESSENCE OF HUMAN INTELLIGENCE IS TO FORGE LINKS; TO GO BEYOND THE GIVEN; TO SEE PATTERN, RELATIONSHIPS, CONTEXT."

--MARILYN FERGUSON

CHAPTER SEVEN: EVALUATING

It is a safe bet to say that no person could directly experience all the things he or she needs to know. Much experience is passed on by word of mouth and through books, and each person must judge the accuracy and value of these ideas. To make a judgment requires an ability to evaluate data, and thus you can see how central to our daily experience the act of evaluating or making judgments can be. In each minute of existence, we are called upon to make many evaluative judgments. Some are of relatively minor consequence, but others can have life-changing significance for ourselves and others.

Philosophers tell us that there are two kinds of judgments: *necessary judgments* and *contingent judgments. When we say that "a triangle has three* sides" or "two plus two equals four in the base ten number system," the facts have no reasonable alternatives, and we judge these statements as true. Because there are no other reasonable alternatives to the facts, we must view these determinations as *necessary judgments.*

However, if we say, "food satisfies hunger," the truth of this statement depends on other facts and interpretations. The person eating the food could be ill and unable to digest the food, or the person could be suffering from a neurosis in which he or she eats to satisfy emotional needs and is never full or free from hunger no matter how much he or she eats. Judgments of this nature that are subject to interpretation or that can be contradicted are said to be *contingent judgments.*

The judgments that influence our lives the most generally are *contingent judgments,* that call for an interpretation of data. Most of our *beliefs* are types of contingent judgments based on what experienced people tell us or upon events that are not easily proved. For example, we believe that George Washington was the first President of the United States, but, since we could not directly experience this fact, we rely on what historians tell us. We recognize, too, in this type of judgment, the possibility for error and the fact that if new data surfaced about George Washington we might make a different judgment in the future.

Our *opinions* operate in a similar fashion, in that *opinions* are really a weak form of belief. When we have an opinion, we usually wait for more facts before making a firm judgment. We may have an opinion, as your textbook indicates, that the Yugo is a fine car, but our opinion might change after we have taken the Yugo out for a test drive or read the latest car magazines on the Yugo's durability and dependability.

Since so many of our judgments are contingent judgments and depend upon our ability to interpret and evaluate data, evaluation is an important aspect of human intelligence. Learning to evaluate with greater precision and a higher degree of accuracy can be one of the most important skills you acquire during your academic training. Your composition course will greatly facilitate the acquisition of this skill since rhetoric emphasizes an assessment of how language is used to influence beliefs and shape public opinion.

Exercise #1

Reflect for a moment upon the ways that you make judgments and formulate opinions and beliefs. What do you think are the strongest factors that influence your judgments and beliefs? When you find yourself in a difference of opinion or of belief with another person, what steps do you ordinarily undertake to resolve those differences? Do you consider yourself an open-minded individual receptive to new ideas, or do you feel you are pretty set in your opinions and beliefs? Why do you think that might be? Do you feel most people are fairly open-minded or closed-minded in their beliefs? Why do you think so?

Evaluation depends upon *evidence*, and evidence consists of facts or interpretations of facts that you use to support your arguments. A *fact* is information that can be verified; an *interpretation* is a personal judgment made on the basis of facts. Facts may remain constant, but interpretations may vary. This is a fact of human existence.

Factual evidence consists of *examples* and *statistics*. *Both examples and statistics can be derived from* your own experience and from research that you do for an assignment. Examples are specific instances that support larger generalizations. Examples are used best when they are representative and not stereotypical or slanted. To evaluate fairly, you must use your examples fairly. If you see one work-study student who is not doing a good job on your campus, it is neither fair nor accurate to argue that all work-study students are lazy and incompetent. This viewpoint seems highly self-evident, but you'd be surprised how many people jump to hasty conclusions or overlook important facts in making their evaluations of others.

An example gives a specific instance, while *statistics* are numerical summaries of specific instances or pieces of information. Statistics can be very convincing in an evaluation. If you find, for example, that 87% of all Yugo owners were dissatisfied with their "frequency of repair rate" for their cars in 1987, this can be a much more convincing piece of data than telling the example of Joe Jones who had his Yugo in the shop 291 days out of 365 days last year. While Joe's case is part of the statistics you are quoting, the impact of the larger numbers attached to the statistics is more powerful and convincing than the narrating of the one case or instance Joe represents. Statistics, therefore, can give your reader a better understanding of some issues than a single example can. A reader can always be uncertain of exactly how representative your example is--after all, Joe Jones might be the only dissatisfied Yugo owner in America. Statistics, though, put your information into perspective and allow for comparisons to be made. In a similar fashion, statistics give readers the impression that they are getting a cross-section of opinion rather than possibly an isolated viewpoint.

Statistics, of course, like all rhetorical techniques, can be used incorrectly and interpreted in a distorted fashion. You might conduct a poll in which you discover that 91% of the people interviewed in Pleasant Valley are opposed to abortion, but neglect to tell your readers that you only interviewed people on their way out from church services on Sunday morning. Your statistical survey is not representative, and so all interpretations of your data are suspect.

In all instances when you are evaluating, there is a fine line between making your case and being unfair. Often we see such instances of unfairness during political years when opponents are evaluating each other's records for the public. One person running for public office might accuse his opponent of being soft on defense because he voted against a bill to increase government spending on a new missile system. The truth is, though, that if the opponent would look at all of the senator's voting record, he would find that the senator has been quite consistently a strong advocate of defense spending. His objection to the missile system was based upon government waste in spending, since the firm that would get the contract to produce the missile system had proven to be quite wasteful of taxpayers' money over the years. Thus, the senator was not opposing defense spending but only government waste. A fair interpretation of his vote against the missile system would include an assessment of the reasons for his vote, not just the vote itself. The vote is a fact, or a datum, that is subject to a range of interpretations. The best of those interpretations will be accurate and fair, and the worst will be distorted and unfair.

The slanted use of statistics or of descriptive terms is not confined only to politics; advertising has its fair share of distortions. Several years ago, a company that manufactured a cranberry drink was cited by the government for distorted advertising when the company claimed that its cranberry cocktail contained "more food energy" than orange juice or grapefruit juice and was therefore a better choice as a breakfast drink to start one's day with. What the consumer heard in "more food energy" was probably something like more vitamins and minerals, when actually all the phrase meant was that the cranberry drink had more *calories* than orange juice or grapefruit juice. While the company technically did not lie, since calories do provide food energy, it certainly phrased its pitch in such a way that consumers would be likely to interpret its ads in a favorable manner. Certainly in a much more favorable manner than if the company had said, "Our cranberry cocktail is a better choice for breakfast because it has more calories than orange juice or grapefruit juice." Probably not many consumers would have been drawn to a sales pitch like that!

Advertisements are excellent examples of how the interpretations we place upon data are much more important than the facts or data themselves. One company that encourages people to buy land in its development sends out postcards announcing that the person named on the card has won $10,000 guaranteed. If the person comes out to the development, he or she can claim the prize, no strings attached. When excited and unsuspecting individuals do arrive, they discover that they have indeed won $10,000, but not in U.S. currency. Their prize is $10,000 in

Monopoly money. Again, the company technically has not lied, but it has successfully depended upon the types of interpretations and evaluations individuals will place upon data, and it has used that factor to its advantage.

Group Exercise #1

Let the class bring in examples of advertisements that they feel rely upon interpretations of slogans, pictorial representations, and data that favorable to the product and perhaps misleading to the consumer. Let the class also discuss the process of interpretation and evaluation that goes on for consumers in responding to advertising. In what ways do advertisers depend upon consumers' abilities to evaluate data favorably and in accord with what the advertisers have anticipated?

Advertisements provide us with a good means for understanding interpretations and evaluations and how these two judgment factors are integrally related. If we look at an advertisement for an automobile, for example, in which a beautiful young woman dressed in an elegant evening gown is stretched across the hood of a sports car, what types of evaluative judgments will most of us place upon the automobile. Since the advertisement seems to be pitched mostly to men, is it possible men will associate the car with the woman and begin to form in their minds an interpretation that having XYZ sports car will attract women of beauty and elegance? Is it possible once this interpretation has been made that the evaluation that follows will be," XYZ is a wonderful sports car and I'd love to have one?" The odds are very high, at least, that the evaluation of the sports car will be highly favorable.

And therein lies the catch, since the presence of the female in the advertisement is no guarantee that XYZ sports car is truly a well-made vehicle. In fact, such advertising gimmicks might be needed to sell the car because there is very little positive data to include about the car's performance or durability. Since being attractive to attractive women is a male fantasy that can be counted upon to strike many emotional cords in men, the use of a beautiful model to sell XYZ sports car becomes an advertising device that encourages men to place a particular interpretation upon the product that is being sold. The assumption is that both the interpretation and the evaluation that follows will be favorable to the product.

The process of judgment the consumer goes through in this example might run something like this:

*Attractive women are desirable. [A societal ideal and evaluation].

*I would like to have attractive women attracted to me. [A personal incorporation into one's own value schema of a societal ideal].

125

*The woman in this advertisement is attractive. [A personal evaluation based, in part, upon societal definitions and norms].

*The woman in this advertisement seems to like XYZ sports cars. [A personal interpretation].

*If I owned an XYZ sports car, women like this might be attracted to me. [A personal interpretation].

In all truth, the only hard data or facts given in the advertisement are that a woman in an evening gown is stretched out upon the hood of XYZ sports car. All other reactions to this advertisement, including even the judgment of whether or not the woman is attractive, are matters of interpretation and evaluation.

If we moved two concepts--(1) the woman is attractive and (2) XYZ is a good sports car--out of the advertisement and into the realm of discussion or debate, how would you go about structuring a line of reasoning to support each of these evaluations? The first step, as in all evaluative writings, is to establish what is known as a *standard of judgment*. Statements like, "The woman is attractive" and "XYZ is a good sports car," do not have much meaning without a standard of judgment to be applied. In essence, the standard of judgment responds to the issue of *because*. It fills in the line of reasoning in this fashion: "The woman is attractive because she is physically fit." Thus, being physically fit becomes your standard of judgment for attractiveness in women. If this is the case, the opposite must also apply, in that women who are not physically fit are also not attractive.

In terms of the sports car, you could define a standard of judgment in this manner: "XYZ is a good sports car because it is dependable." Dependability becomes your standard of judgment, and the assumption is that dependable cars are good, while undependable cars are bad, or of low quality.

Obviously, as you can imagine, standards of judgment are themselves subject to interpretation and debate. If you said that the woman was attractive because she has red hair, those who do not think red hair is particularly attractive might take issue with you. If you said XYZ was a good sports car because it was dependable, those who think speed and performance are more important in a sports car than dependability might take issue with you, too. The important thing is to define a standard of judgment that makes sense for the line of reasoning you are going to pursue, and then to stick with that standard of judgment and that line of reasoning throughout your essay. If you anticipate objections to your standard of judgment or your line of reasoning, you can deal with them in the refutation section of your essay in which you consider and counter opposing arguments.

Exercise #2

Establish a standard of judgment for each of the following statements:

1. The college I attend is an excellent school.

2. Professor Becker is a good teacher.

3. The tax increase recently approved for Happy Valley will be very beneficial.

4. Premarital sex is not a good idea.

5. Premarital sex is a good idea.

6. Paradise Cafe is the best restaurant in town.

7. This novel is the worst book I've ever read.

8. Gun control is a good idea for society to pursue.

9. Gun control is not a good idea for society to pursue.

10. A college education is valuable in today's world.

11. Pornography corrupts a society's values.

12. Money can't buy happiness.

Exercise #3

Consider the following excerpt from "Pragmatism," an essay by William James, and evaluate the merit or truth of what James is saying. Do you agree or disagree with his perspective? Why or why not? What relevance might James' views have to your study of evaluation?

Truth lives . . . for the most part on a credit system. Our thoughts and beliefs "pass," so long as nothing challenges them, just as banknotes pass so long as nobody refuses them. But this all points to direct face-to-face verifications somewhere, without which the fabric of truth collapses like a financial system with no cash basis whatever. You accept my verification of one thing, I yours of another. We trade on each other's truth. But beliefs verified concretely by *somebody* are the posts of the whole superstructure.

Exercise #4

William James states that "beliefs verified concretely by *somebody* are the posts of the whole superstructure [of Truth]." Based upon your study of evaluation, what methods, in your opinion, would seem to work best at verifying beliefs? What are some methods you might suggest that could be used to verify facts or beliefs? How would these methods work, and what would be their limitations?

Exercise #5

Consider the following excerpt from "Inference Peddling," an essay by Robert Fuerst that appeared in the March 1979 issue of *Psychology Today*. Even though Fuerst's essay is humorous, what point is he making about how people draw inferences and make evaluations?

At any large convention of psychologists, you may hear some speaker tell the story about a psychologist who trained a cockroach to jump at a verbal command. After a period of conditioning, the roach invariably jumped when the psychologist said, "Jump." One day, the psychologist pulled a leg off the roach and then said, "Jump," and the roach jumped. He pulled another leg off the roach and again the roach jumped at the verbal command "Jump." The process was continued until the last leg was removed from the roach, and this time when the psychologist commanded, "Jump," the roach did not budge. In reporting this experimental work, the psychologist wrote, "When a cockroach loses all of its legs, it becomes stone deaf."

Free Writing #1

Have you ever found yourself in a situation similar to the one Fuerst describes for the psychologist in which you drew incorrect inferences from your experiences? Perhaps these instances were humorous, like Fuerst's tale. Perhaps they had more significant and lasting consequences. Whatever the dimensions of your experience, write about a time when you drew incorrect inferences/conclusions about an experience in your life. If the episode did not actually happen to you, write about a story or an even that you have heard about.

While it is possible that during your college education you might be asked to evaluate an object (like a painting in an art history class) or a person (like a political figure in your history class), by and large the what you will be asked to evaluate the most are ideas. In fact, some people view the essence of a liberal arts education as instilling in the individual the capacity to weigh, consider, and fairly assess concepts and ideas.

How does one go about the process of evaluating ideas? First, of course, a standard of judgment must be worked out. It is impossible to evaluate ideas in the abstract. The standard of judgment gives both a context for evaluation and a method. Second, ideas must have a type of internal consistency or internal logic. If a writer's ideas contradict each other, the odds are that he or she will have a very weak essay that will be evaluated as a poor essay. Third, ideas that are not purely metaphysical or speculative (and even these at times) are often judged on the value of their practical application, or on the basis of how much of reality they explain. Ideas that explain a great deal about the world around us and that cover a large number of instances or examples generally are thought superior to ideas that explain very little and only apply to a few select instances.

In terms of evaluating the merit of an author's ideas, consider the following passage from French philosopher Simone Weil.

If we concentrate our attention on trying to solve a problem of geometry, and if at the end of an hour we are no nearer to doing so than at the beginning, we have nevertheless been making progress each minute of that hour in another more mysterious dimension. Without our knowing or feeling it, this apparently barren effort has brought more light into the soul. The result will one day . . . very likely be felt in some department of the intelligence in no way connected with mathematics. Perhaps he who made the unsuccessful effort will one day be able to grasp the beauty of a line of Racine more vividly on account of it . . . . Every time that a human being succeeds in making an effort of attention with the sole idea of increasing his grasp of truth, he acquires a greater aptitude for grasping it, even if his effort produces no visible fruit. An Eskimo story explains the origin of light as follows: "In the eternal darkness, the crow, unable to find any food, longed for light, and the earth was illumined." If there is a real desire, if the thing desired is really light, the desire for light produces it. There is a real desire when there is an effort of attention.

Part of evaluating the ideas in this passage depends upon our ability to locate the central or main idea (thesis) and its supporting ideas (proofs). To locate the thesis, we must first identify the topic that Weil is dealing with. A topic is a general category of idea (like economics, politics, society), while a thesis represents a point to be made about a topic.

The topic of Weil's essay is rather easy to deduce, since most of the essay deals with how people learn. We might state, thus, that her essay deals with learning theory or with education, and then we must focus our interest even more narrowly and find the thesis Weil advocates in dealing with her topic.

To accomplish this end, it is important for us to realize that essays generally are composed of exposition (or necessary background information--also called an introduction), a thesis, and proofs, supports, or examples for that thesis. A conclusion is an optional part of an essay, but most essays have some sort of concluding paragraph or paragraphs that tie the ideas in the essay together into a general insight.

In analyzing Weil's statements, we must first determine what is expository information and what is a thesis. Expository statements generally give information, while a thesis presents a statement that can be debated or argued. A look at the excerpt from Weil, sentence by sentence, will reveal this process more clearly.

Sentence #1, "If we concentrate our attention on trying to solve a problem of geometry, and if at the end of an hour we are no nearer to doing so than at the beginning, we have nevertheless been making progress each minute of that hour in another more mysterious dimension," seems too limited to be a thesis, since it focuses upon one learning task only--a geometry problem. The odds are that this sentence is an expository statement because it is laying the ground work for a more general statement (or thesis) later on.

Sentence #2, "Without our knowing or feeling it, this apparently barren effort has brought more light into the soul," is a further explanation (and exemplification) of Sentence #1 and seems an unlikely candidate for a thesis statement that can be argued in the affirmative or the negative. This is a good rule of thumb to follow, in that sentences that serve as examples or further explanations of ideas developed in previous sentences are rarely thesis statements. They are exactly what they appear to be--examples and further explanations.

Sentence #3, "The result will one day . . . very likely be felt in some department of the intelligence in no way connected with mathematics," is again a continuation and further exemplification of the ideas presented in Sentence #1. Since it is an explanatory sentence and since it deals with the narrow instance or example of mathematics within the whole of all education and learning, it, too, seems an unlikely candidate for a thesis statement for all the reasons presented about Sentence #2.

Sentence #4, "Perhaps he who made the unsuccessful effort will one day be able to grasp the beauty of a line of Racine more vividly on account of it . . . . ," is obviously a further explanation of the ideas raised in Sentences 1-3, and, since it focuses upon a specific example (seeing the beauty in a line of Racine), is not broad enough to encompass the high level of generalization usually contained in a thesis statement.

Sentence #5, "Every time that a human being succeeds in making an effort of attention with the sole idea of increasing his grasp of truth, he acquires a greater aptitude for grasping it, even if his effort produces no visible fruit," seems an excellent candidate for the thesis of this excerpt. For one, it represents a shift in subject and thus is no longer a further exemplification of ideas in Sentences 1-4.

Second, it encompasses a broad general statement rather than a specific and more limited (narrow) example. Third, the general statement that it makes is one that can be debated in that it can be responded to in the affirmative or the negative.

If we are still uncertain as to whether Sentence #5 is our thesis, process of elimination will help us resolve the dilemma. If no other candidates surface in the remainder of the excerpt, Sentence #5 has to be the thesis.

Sentence #6, "An Eskimo story explains the origin of light as follows: "In the eternal darkness, the crow, unable to find any food, longed for light, and the earth was illumined," is an example that serves to clarify and support the idea presented in Sentence #5, so it is highly unlikely that an example will be our thesis.

Sentence #7, "If there is a real desire, if the thing desired is really light, the desire for light produces it," is a summary statement that explains the example given in the Eskimo story. As a summary of what has come before, it is not a thesis statement.

Sentence #8, "There is a real desire when there is an effort of attention," is broad enough to serve as a thesis statement, but it is a summary statement for the example in Sentences 6-7. Since it is summarizing a previous sentence rather than presenting a new idea of its own, it is a less likely candidate for the thesis of this excerpt than is Sentence #5.

Determining what is the thesis in this excerpt is a process of interpretation; determining the merit, value, or "truth" of that thesis is a process of evaluation. The question then becomes, "How does one evaluate a thesis?" The response is that such an evaluation cannot be done in a vacuum. In other words, a standard of judgment must be articulated.

Are we, for example, going to apply pragmatism as a standard of judgment and see if what Weil says is practical and applicable in terms of our view of the world? Or are we going to apply the "umbrella theory" as our standard in asserting that this statement explains and illuminates more instances than it eliminates or cannot explain? Another possibility is that we can use common sense or everyday experience as our standard and see if Weil's thesis is consistent with our experience of the world. Whatever is the determining factor, we cannot ascertain the "truth" value of any statement or thesis until we articulate a standard of judgment.

For the sake of our discussion, let us apply the standard of common experience to the thesis statement, "Every time that a human being succeeds in making an effort of attention with the sole idea of increasing his grasp of truth, he acquires a greater aptitude for grasping it, even if his effort produces no visible fruit." For one, we could start with the statement, "every time," which is a highly broad generalization. Nothing, we could argue, occurs all the time, every time. Citing one instance in which what Weil predicts would not, in fact, occur goes a long way toward questioning the truth value of what Weil is suggesting.

Continuing on with our line of reasoning from everyday experience, has it been your experience that every time you have applied yourself toward learning and the "grasping" of truth that, even if that one effort did not work out, your ability to understand and to grasp truth was enhanced nonetheless? Do you feel it is true that if you spend a weekend trying to learn calculus and fail miserably in the attempt that you nonetheless learned about learning and that this "learning about learning" (or, perhaps, learning *how* to learn) will someday pay dividends that you cannot even now anticipate?

If you say yes, you then affirm Weil's thesis and can write in support of it by drawing upon your own experiences as examples. If you say no, then you negate Weil's thesis and can write against it, again by drawing upon your own experience to disprove Weil's views. In either instance, pro or con, you are evaluating the "truth" value (or validity) of Weil's statement. And this is exactly the point at which your essay would begin if you were assigned the writing task of evaluating the ideas contained in this passage.

Often teachers will give an excerpt like Weil's and state at the end "Discuss" or "Do you agree with Weil's views? Why or why not?" Basically what they are asking, however they phrase it, is for an evaluation of the merit of the ideas presented in the excerpt. "Evaluate the ideas in this passage and tell me what you think of them" is what the instructors are saying, and the process you can follow to carry out this task will involve interpreting what is the thesis of the excerpt, what standard of judgment should be applied, and what is the overall merit (or value) of the ideas proposed in the passage.

Group Exercise #2

Following the model developed in the analysis of the excerpt from Simone Weil, evaluate the ideas contained in the following selections. Be sure to (1) locate the thesis for each selection; (2) establish a standard of judgment for assessing the thesis' claims; and (3) evaluate the merit of the ideas proposed in each selection. If a selection initially seems difficult to comprehend, you may wish to summarize or paraphrase the selection as a starting point for your discussion.

1. Alfred North Whitehead, *Adventures of Ideas*

In any human society, one fundamental idea tingeing every detail of activity is the general conception of the status of the individual members of that group, considered apart from any special preeminence. In such societies as they emerge into civilization, the members recognize each other as individuals exercising the enjoyment of emotions, passions, comforts and discomforts, perceptions, hopes, fears, and purposes. Also there are powers of intellectual understanding involving discrimination of details of characters, judgments of "true or false," and of "beautiful or ugly," and of "good or bad." We pass our lives vaguely and flittingly entertaining groups of such experiences, and we attribute like ways of existence to others.

But in the early stages of civilization such experiences and beliefs are mere matters of course. They provoke no abrupt reflective reaction isolating them for thoughtful introspection. Accordingly there is no modification of habit arising from the valuation of human beings as such. Thus the various members of a society find themselves cherishing each other, destroying, obeying or commanding, as the case may be. There is a communal organization, and there are beliefs about it slowly forming themselves into explanations.

We are to discuss the later phases when civilization has reached its modern height, a period of three thousand years at the most. Thinkers have now arisen. The notion of duty has dawned and received some definition. Above all the notion of a psyche--that is, of a mind--has dawned. In its first phase of gradual emergence, this great notion was instinctively used as a master-key to make intelligible the baffling occurrences of nature. The two most obvious characteristics of Nature, write Lytton Strachey, are loveliness and power. The beauty dawned later upon human intelligence than did its power. Also in early phases of thought the powers of nature became the minds of Nature--minds bestial, ruthless, and yet placable. In all stages of civilization the popular gods represent the more primitive brutalities of the tribal life. The progress of religion is defined by the denunciation of gods. The keynote of idolatry is contentment with the prevalent gods.

2. Stephen W. Hawking, *A Brief History of Time*

The eventual goal of science is to provide a single theory that describes the whole universe. However, the approach most scientists actually follow is to separate the problem into two parts. FIrst, there are the laws that tell us how the universe changes with time. (If we know what the universe is like at any one time, these physical laws tell us how it will look at any later time.) Second, there is the question of the initial state of the universe. Some people feel that science should be concerned with only the first part; they regard the question of the initial situation as a matter for metaphysics or religion. They would say that God, being omnipotent, could have started the universe off any way he wanted. That may be so, but in that case he also could have made it develop in a completely arbitrary way. Yet it appears that he chose to make it evolve in a very regular way according to certain laws. It therefore seems equally reasonable to suppose that there are also laws governing the initial state.

It turns out to be very difficult to devise a theory to describe the universe all in one go. Instead, we break the problem up into bits and invent a number of partial theories. Each of these partial theories describes and predicts a certain limited class of observations, neglecting the effects of other quantities, or representing them by simple sets of numbers. It may be that this approach is completely wrong. If everything in the universe depends on everything else in a fundamental way, it might be impossible to get close to a full solution by investigating parts of the problem in isolation. Nevertheless, it is certainly the way that we have made progress in the past. The classic example again is the Newtonian theory of gravity, which tells us that the gravitational force between two bodies depends only on one number associated with each body, its mass, but otherwise independent of what the bodies are made of. Thus one does not need to have a theory of the structure and constitution of the sun and the planets in order to calculate their orbits.

3. Stanley A. Aronowitz and Henry A. Giroux, *Education Under Siege*

After nearly two decades of benign neglect, schools are once more the subject of an intense national debate. In the recent past, discussion has centered on three issues: whether schools can be the central institution for achieving racial and sexual equality; in higher education, whether the traditional liberal arts curricula are still "relevant" to a changing labor market; and whether the authoritarian classroom stifles the creativity of young children or, conversely, how permissiveness has resulted in a general lowering of educational achievement. All of these issues are still with us, but they have been subsumed under a much larger question: how to make schools adequate to a changing economic, political and ideological environment?

As has been the case with most public issues in American society, the conservatives have seized the initiative and put liberals and progressives on the defensive. Their arguments have force not only because conservatism has become dominant in the ideological realm, but because their critique seems to correspond to the actual situation. In the first place, conservatives have joined radical critics in announcing that the schools have failed to educate, a perception shared by most parents, teachers, and administrators. And, secondly, they have coupled their point with a clear analysis of the causes and a program for curing the affliction. To be sure, their analysis is by no means original or intellectually challenging. They have taken their cue from radical critics who claim that schooling is merely an adjunct to the labor market. But, unlike the left, conservatives criticize the schools for failing to fulfill this function. With some exceptions, they are happy to jettison the traditional liberal vision that schools must be responsible for transmitting western cultural and intellectual traditions. Instead, they have repeated the 1960s radical attack that schools are not relevant to students' lives. However, at a time when nearly everyone is anxious about his/her place in a rapidly shifting job market, relevance has come to mean little else than job preparation. While many jobs require applicants to know how to read and write and to possess skills for specialized employment, few employers require mastery or even familiarity with literary canon, the arts, and music, much less a secure command of history and the social sciences. Conservatives demand "excellence," by which they usually mean that schools should offer more rigorous science and math curriculum--a notion in keeping with the conservative idea that the mastery of techniques is equivalent to progress. Their language of "achievement," "excellence," "discipline," and "goal orientation" really means vocational education or, in their most traditional mode, a return to the authoritarian classroom armed with the three Rs curriculum.

4. Theodor Adorno, *Aesthetic Theory*

Art is the social antithesis of society. The constitution of the domain of art resembles the constitution of an inner space of ideas in the individual. Both areas intersect in the concept of sublimation. Hence it is natural and promising to attempt to conceptualize art in terms of some theory of psychic life.

A comparison between an anthropological theory of human constants and a psychoanalytic one would seem to favour the latter. But caution is in order: psychoanalysis is better suited to explain purely psychic phenomena than aesthetic ones. According to

psychoanalytic theory, works of art are essentially projections of the unconscious. Psychoanalysis thus puts the emphasis on the individual producer of art and the interpretation of aesthetic content as psychic content, to the detriment of categories of form. What psychoanalysis does when it turns to the analysis of art is to transfer the banaustic sensitivity of the therapist to such unlikely objects as Leonardo and Baudelaire. It is important to debunk such studies, which are frequently offshoots of the biographical genre, in no uncertain terms; for despite their stress on sex they are hopelessly philistine in conception, dismissing as neurotics men of art who in fact merely objectified in their work the negativity of life.

5. Dorothy Leigh Sayers, "Are Women Human?"

The question of "sex equality" is, like all questions affecting human relationships, delicate and complicated. It cannot be settled by loud slogans or hard-and-fast assertions like "a woman is as good as a man"--or "woman's place is in the home"-- or "women ought not to take men's jobs." The minute one makes such assertions, one finds one has to qualify them. "A woman is as good as a man" is as meaningless as to say, "a Kaffir is as good as a Frenchman" or "a poet is as good as an engineer" or "an elephant is as good as a racehorse"--it means nothing whatever until you add: "at doing what?" In a religious sense, no doubt, the Kaffir is as valuable in the yes of God as a Frenchman--but the average Kaffir is probably less skilled in literary criticism than the average Frenchman, and the average Frenchman less skilled than the average Kaffir in tracing the spoor of big game. There might be exceptions on either side: it is largely a matter of heredity and education. When we balance the poet against the engineer, we are faced with a fundamental difference of temperament--so that here our question is complicated by the enormous social problem whether poetry or engineering is "better" for the State, or for humanity in general. There may be people who would like a world that was all engineers or all poets--but most of us would like to have a certain number of each; though here again, we should all differ about the desirable proportion of engineering to poetry . . . . When we come to the elephant and the racehorse, we come down to bed-rock physical differences--the elephant would make a poor showing in the Derby, and the unbeaten Eclipse himself would be speedily eclipsed by an elephant when it came to hauling logs.

That is so obvious that it hardly seems worth saying. But it is the mark of all movements, however well-intentioned, that their pioneers tend, by much lashing of themselves into excitement, to lose sight of the obvious. In reaction against the age-old slogan, "woman is the weaker vessel," or the still more offensive, "woman is a divine creature," we have, I think, allowed ourselves to drift into asserting that "a woman is as good as a man," without always pausing to think what exactly we mean by that. What, I feel, we ought to mean is something so obvious that it is apt to escape attention altogether, viz: not that every woman is, in virtue of her sex, as strong, clever, artistic, level-headed, industrious and so forth as any man that can be mentioned; but, that a woman is just as much an ordinary human being as a man, with the same individual preferences, and with just as much right to the tastes and preferences of an individual.

6. Alice Walker, "In Search of Our Mothers' Garden"

When the poet Jean Toomer walked through the South in the early twenties, he discovered a curious thing: black women whose spirituality was so intense, so deep, so *unconscious*, that they were themselves unaware of the richness they held. They stumbled blindly through their lives: creatures so abused and mutilated in body, so dimmed and confused by pain, that they considered themselves unworthy even of hope. In the selfless abstractions their bodies became to the men who used them, they became more than "sexual objects," more even than mere women: they became "Saints." Instead of being perceived as whole persons, their bodies became shrines: what was thought to be their minds became temples suitable for worship. These crazy Saints stared out at the world, wildly like lunatics--or quietly, like suicides, and the "God" that was in their gaze was as mute as a great stone.

Who were these Saints? These crazy, loony, pitiful women?

Some of them, without a doubt, were our mothers and grandmothers.

In the still heat of the post-Reconstruction South, this is how they seemed to Jean Toomer: exquisite butterflies trapped in an evil honey, toiling away their lives in an era, a century, that did not acknowledge them, except as "the *mule* of the world." They dreamed dreams that no one knew--not even themselves, in any coherent fashion--and saw visions no one could understand. They wandered or sat about the countryside crooning lullabies to ghosts, and drawing the mother of Christ in charcoal on courthouse walls.

Choose an idea from one of the preceding selections that stands out in your mind as insightful or intriguing and free write for ten or fifteen minutes about that idea. Of all the ideas in the preceding selections, what made this idea so interesting and important for you?

Point/Counterpoint: Considering Opposing Arguments

1. Mark says to his friend Lee, "I find it difficult to write evaluations. My sense of whether something is good or bad or has any merit or validity at all is very personal and subjective. It's mostly how I *feel* about something pro or con. How can I put that into words in such a way that people can even understand what I'm saying, much less agree with me?"

How would you respond to Mark's statements?

2. Some theorists argue that evaluation is not only impossible, it is destructive because all acts of evaluation are colored by one's personal prejudices and cultural and societal influences. No one can evaluate anything, especially the hard work and efforts of another, without bringing into his or her judgments the prejudices and biases of personal experience and cultural stereotypes.

How would you respond to this perspective? Do you agree or disagree? Why or why not?

3. One of the most common aspects of evaluation that you, as a student, would have personal knowledge of is grading. All grading depends upon the development of a standard of judgment. It would be impossible to grade without some sense, some standard of judgment, for what constituted quality, effectiveness, or "good work" in a person's effort or achievement.

Develop what you think would be a good standard of judgment for the evaluation of writing assignments and develop a set of grading criteria that would enable you to apply your standard in the assessment of student papers. If, after you had developed your standard of judgment and your criteria, someone told you that your viewpoint was too limited in perspective and too narrow in application, how would you respond?

4. Gather up a set of assignments that you have been given in your high school or college courses and evaluate these assignments on how clearly they have been formulated. In other words, evaluate them on the basis of whether they provide adequate clues about the shape and content your writing should take and if they give you clear information about how you should proceed with the assignment.

After you have completed phase one of this assignment, develop a set of criteria and a standard of judgment for evaluating the instructions given in assignments and the merit of what cognitive tasks assignments ask students to perform.

Based upon your experience of assessing assignments, how would you respond to the viewpoint that most assignments look only for a restatement of what the teacher already knows and do not, in general, encourage original thinking from students?

This exercise, too, is a form of an assignment. Do you think it has encouraged you to original thinking or only to express what you already know? Why might that be?

5. Evaluate the model and process of evaluation that you have been given by your textbook and your workbook. Do you agree with this view of evaluation? What aspects would you change, enhance, elaborate upon, or question? Do you have an alternative model that you would propose? How would this model differ from the ones in your texts? In what ways would it be superior to the ones in your texts?

6. One assumption of a critical thinking approach to writing instruction is that thinking skills build upon each other, that the skill of observing details, for example, will complement the skill of description or of investigation, which will, in turn, complement the skill of argumentation and persuasion. Do you agree with this approach? Do you think intellectual skills build upon, influence, and enhance each other? If so, how do you see the skills you have learned in other chapters of your texts, like observing, remembering, etc., fitting in with and enhancing the skill of evaluation? What other intellectual skills do you think evaluation might help in strengthening and developing? Why do you think so?

SUMMARY AND ASSESSMENT PAGE

What ideas from *CHAPTER SEVEN: EVALUATING* (in either your textbook or your workbook) helped you the most with your writing? What ideas or techniques did you hope to get from this chapter but did not? What steps do you intend to take to learn those ideas or techniques?

"ALL MEN BY NATURE DESIRE TO LEARN"

--ARISTOTLE

CHAPTER EIGHT: PROBLEM SOLVING

As your textbook indicates, problem solving operates on the assumption that you must first be able to prove that a problem exists before you can propose a solution for that problem. This seems a very obvious idea, but you would be amazed at how many students start their papers with the assumption that everyone thinks the same as they do and therefore sees the same problems that they do. Two premises to be aware of here: (1) not everyone agrees that what you think is a problem *is* a problem; and (2) even if others agree with you that a problem exists, they still might not be seeing the problem or its potential solution from the same angle that you do.

The (exciting) challenge is that #1 and #2 are where *communication* comes in. Your ability to use language to your advantage, to persuade your audience, will be vital skills here and skills that you can work to your benefit. Without effective language skills, your problem truly *is* your problem, for you will be unable to convince others of your point of view or to rally support when you need it most.

What idea/meaning comes to your mind when you think of the term *problem*?

What critical thinking skills do you think are required for problem solving?

Group Exercise #1

Bring to class, from newspaper and magazine articles, examples of writings that define a problem and propose a solution. Using the criteria established for you in your textbook, evaluate the essays, paying particular attention to: (1) how well the writer defined the problem; and (2) the criteria used for proposing solutions to the problem.

Let individuals (or groups) propose alternative solutions to the problem and make as convincing a case as possible for the position that their solution is better than the original one proposed.

A good idea to remember about problem solving is that defining the problem for your audience is often easier than getting your audience's attention about that problem. Many readers may agree that homelessness is a problem in America, but many may also not want to hear about the depressing statistic associated with "street people." They would prefer to ignore the problem or at least not focus upon it. Capturing the audience's attention will require from you a masterful command of writing techniques, including your ability to explain through examples, to describe, and to narrate.

The French have a saying, *plus ca change, pluc c'est la meme chose*" [the more things change, the more they stay the same], and this represents many people's attitude toward problem solving. They have a type of "burn out" on listening to problems or in ever believing again that there are solutions since they have seen too many good ideas fail and have become inured in their cynicism.

Capturing their attention will be a unique challenge, and enlisting their efforts an even more herculean task. That is why devising appropriate rhetorical strategies is crucial to problem solving, for it is extremely important to know one's audience and to know one's form of approach.

Actually, the problems you might face in such an undertaking have already been anticipated by Aristotle, a Greek philosopher and rhetorician who saw that arguments, to be effective, must address both the rational and the emotional sides of an audience. The philosophical/rhetorical tradition of Aristotle focused upon rhetoric as "the faculty of observing in any given case the available means of persuasion."

For Aristotle, there were five means of persuasion, three of which were rhetorical, or within the realm of language to persuade. The two non-verbal means involved threat or bribery, while the three verbal means available to the writer or speaker were *logos*, *pathos*, and *ethos*. *Essentially, if my act of persuasion (what I wanted you* to do) was for you to get up and close the door for me, I would have five means of persuasion at my disposal. I could threaten you--"Close the door or I'll hit you!" "Close the door or you're grounded for a week and no spending money either." "Close the door or you're in big trouble." Or, conversely, I could bribe you--"Close the door and I'll give you $5.00." "Close the door and you can borrow my car next weekend." "Close the door and I'll give you a kiss."

If these two methods failed, I would be dependent upon language to get what I wanted. First, I could appeal to your sense of logic or clear reasoning, which Aristotle called *logos*. "You know, our air conditioning bill for last month was over $150. If you closed the door and kept the cold air from getting out, we might save some on this month's bill." "Close the door so it will be quieter in here and you can get your work done." "Close the door so no one will see in and think of robbing us."

If that didn't work, I could appeal to your emotions, which Aristotle called *pathos*. "Please close the door. You know it's hard for me to get up and down easily these days since I hurt my back." "Please close the door. You know I've done it a thousand times for you." "Please close the door. I had a very hard day at work and I'm exhausted."

My last effort would be an appeal to you based on my character, or *ethos*. "I've never lied to you, have I? It's very important that you close the door." "Trust me. We'll be safer with the door closed." "Based upon my experience with this neighborhood, I think we will avoid unnecessary gossiping and backbiting if we keep the door closed."

In the *Rhetoric*, Aristotle summed up these three rhetorical means of persuasion very nicely:

There are, then, these three means of effecting persuasion. The man who is to be in command of them must, it is clear, be able (1) to reason logically [*logos*], (2) to understand human character and goodness in their various forms [*ethos*], and (3) to understand the emotions--that is, to name them and describe them, to know their causes and the way in which they are excited [*pathos*].

With *ethos*, the writer establishes his or her credibility and good character with the audience; with *pathos*, the writer attempts to appeal to the audience's feelings; and with *logos*, the speaker uses logical proofs and clear reasoning to make the best case possible for his or her position. As Aristotle perceived it, the most powerful of these means was *pathos*, since more people are swayed by their emotions than are responsive to logic or ethical appeals.

Exercise #1

Using Aristotle's schema as a model, construct a problem solving essay in which you define a problem and then endeavor to get your audience to respond to the solutions you propose in terms of *ethos*, *pathos*, and *logos*.

Exercise #2

Do you agree with Aristotle's view that the strongest of the three rhetorical appeals is *pathos*, or the appeal to one's emotions? Why might that be? If this is true and Aristotle is right, how would this influence your view of how to go about writing a problem solving essay?

Free Writing #3

Free write about a time in which you had a problem to solve and you used one of the strategies/approaches described by Aristotle of *logos*, *pathos*, or *ethos*. Was your approach successful? Why or why not? Placed in the same situation again, would you use the same approach or another one? Explain your reasons for your choice.

Exercise #3

Your textbook gives you a set of techniques to consider (perhaps even follow) in writing a problem solving essay.

* Identify and understand your audience.

* Demonstrate that a problem exists.

* Propose a solution that will solve the problem.

* Convince your readers your proposal will work.

Evaluate this set of techniques given to you by your textbook. Do you think this is an effective model for problem solving, or do you feel there are steps left out? Would you modify this set to include other techniques? What would they be?

Group Exercise #2

Identify. Demonstrate. Propose. Convince. Which of these steps in the problem solving process do you think is the most complex? Why? Which do you think is the hardest to do successfully? Why might that be?

Let the class discuss these issues and formulate responses to the questions raised, either in a written assignment or through a class discussion.

Group Exercise #3

For most students, time management is a major problem. Knowing when to study, how to study, how to meet all of one's responsibilities and commitments, and how to handle the rest of one's life while in the midst of going to school and studying represent, for most students, areas in which problem solving techniques might be of great advantage.

Have the class divide into groups and discuss a problem solving approach to the issue of time management for students. Let each group identify the issues involved and then propose a set of techniques for time management that might prove valuable. Let the class also critique, respond to, and suggest ways for improving the proposals presented by each group.

In a certain sense, every form of writing that you do can be viewed as a type of problem solving activity. You certainly must deal with the complexities of the composing process itself, in deciding which strategies you will use for generating

150

ideas, for organizing your material, and for covering all the ideas that you need to in a way that will interest and inform your reader. To a certain extent in this process, you are even dealing with issues of efficiency and how to problem solve here, too, for you do not have unlimited amounts of time in which to structure and create your writing and the odds are that your writing assignment is only one of many tasks, assignments, and life responsibilities you have to deal with in any given period of time.

Another set of problems you address as a writer involves anticipating the needs of your reader and how best to communicate your information to your audience. Knowing what your audience knows and needs to know are issues crucial to the success of your writing. Knowing what level of formality or informality you should incorporate into your writing might mean the difference between a successful and well-received essay, business report, or letter of application and a poor response to your work.

Finally, your own strategies for evaluating your work and revising where needed present a set of problems to be defined and implemented. If you are unable to see the errors and weaknesses in your work, you will have a problem in editing and revising. Similarly, if you do not diagnose and correct these problems you will have a greater problem when your writing is read by informed, literate readers who will not respond to it as positively as you had hoped.

Looking at writing as an exercise in problem solving and as a problem solving activity helps us understand that strategies for solving the problem of writing well are extremely important. Without these strategies, writers can flounder and impede themselves in any stage of the process of writing well. With these strategies, writers become conscious of their own skills, creativity, and insight and become highly goal-oriented to improve their writing.

An awareness of strategies also enables us to know that we have options and choices to make in our writing processes, and that knowledge alone can be very freeing. An awareness of conscious choice gives us a greater sense of control over our writing, as well as taking away the myth that writing well is totally a matter of having talent or not. Talent certainly helps, there's no denying that; but carefully planned and executed strategies help even the weakest of writers to improve and the best of writers to excel.

Taking a problem solving perspective toward writing enables a very important shift in one's consciousness to occur, and that is a movement away from viewing writing as a finished, perfect product toward a perception of writing as a series of conscious acts, choices, and decisions that must be performed. If, while you are writing, your whole consciousness is focused upon making your writing that elusive (and perhaps illusive) perfectly finished essay, you will probably impede your writing by terrifying yourself with unreasonable expectations.

If, however, you start to focus instead upon what you want to achieve with your writing and how best you can do that job by tapping into your own creativity, insight, and skills as a writer, then you are involved not with *product*, but with *process*. And a control over the *process* gives you a much better chance that your *product* will be an accomplished piece of writing that expresses well what you wanted to say.

Exercise #4

What value do you find in viewing writing as a problem solving activity? Do you agree with this view? What strengths and advantages do you find in this perspective? What disadvantages and limitations? What practical differences exist for you between viewing writing as a concern with a finished product and viewing writing as the refinement of critical thinking skills to enable a writer to make increasingly more sophisticated rhetorical judgments and choices?

Free Writing #4

Often descriptions of the writing process make it sound like a very simple and straightforward activity. "Choose a topic, decide on your organizational scheme, write your first draft, revise, edit, and turn in your final draft." Do you think that descriptions of the writing process that make it seem so simple and so easy create problems for most writers? Why or why not?

How would your views of the writing process change if you began to view writing as a thinking process? Would such a view make the idea of writing easier for you, or would it create more problems? **Exercise #5**

Your previous two free writings present different views of the writing process, one emphasizing a straight and predictable linear sequence of activities to follow toward a preconceived goal, and one emphasizing fluidity, an awareness of one's thinking processes, and a sense of writing as recursive and often creatively unpredictable in its results and in its deviance from the writer's preconceived goal. Both of these views of writing can create problems for individual writers. Define the problems both of these perspectives might create for writers and then propose possible solutions. Follow the model presented in your textbook of:

* Identifying and understanding your audience.

* Demonstrating that a problem exists.

* Proposing a solution that will solve the problem.

* Convincing your readers that your proposal will work and that it is better than alternative solutions.

Often, for many writers, the distinction between making a proposal to solve a problem and making an argument is an unclear one. After all, isn't a proposal to solve a problem an argument, and isn't an argument a form of a proposal to solve a problem? Yes, in a way this is true, but, in another way, important distinctions still can be made.

One important difference is that arguments generally deal with what is or already exists, while proposals are addressed to the future and what should be. We may argue over whether *Moby-Dick* is the finest novel ever written, or whether New Age music has any intrinsic value, but we make proposals from a desire to change something--and that suggests an eye toward the future. We are proposing a course of action, and that course of action will materialize in the future.

A second distinction is that proposals deal with concrete issues, while many arguments can be (and often are) over abstractions or abstract principles and ideals. We can argue theoretically, but we must propose specifically and concretely. In our proposal for an end to sexism in American politics, we can theoretically discuss, debate, argue, and evaluate the destructive consequences of sexism in general and in theory, but, when it comes time to propose action, we must move from the abstract and the general to the concrete and specific. We must specifically define sexism, specifically spell out the problem of sexism in American politics and its consequences, and we must specifically propose steps, actions, responses that can be undertaken to resolve this problem. Further, we must specifically indicate why our proposal is better than other solutions that have been presented.

A final distinction is that writing in support of propositions requires a plan of action, a detailed and specific explanation of what should be done. Arguments often do not require such a plan. Arguing over whether *Moby-Dick* is the finest novel ever written does not require a plan of action or a suggestion of what should be done. Instead, it only requires that both debaters be fully informed about their subject and be able reasonably and articulately to defend their positions. This is the defining realm of argumentation. If the debaters decide that because *Moby-Dick* is the finest novel ever written that it should be required reading for all high school students, then the debate has moved out of the realm of argumentation and into the realm of proposing solutions to problems. The problem is that *Moby-Dick*, the finest novel ever written, is not being required for high school students to read. How can we change this situation and make sure that *Moby-Dick* is required reading in the curriculum of all high schools?

By now it should be apparent to you that as much as arguments and proposals differ they also share some striking similarities in the way they collect evidence and present it to others for their assent and affirmation. Both arguments and proposals provide evidence and give examples to support opinions. Both depend upon evidence that is reliable, adequate, and verifiable. Obviously, no one will be swayed by an argument in which insufficient evidence has been presented, nor one in which the evidence is of questionable value and merit. The same will be true of proposals, in that no one will act upon a proposal that presents only sketchy information or, worse yet, presents incorrect evidence or unverifiable claims.

Usually, the types of evidence available for use in both arguments and proposals are *statistics, appeals to authority, personal testimonies, factual references, field research, interviews, and questionnaires.* Each of these types contributes a great deal to the validity and appeal of claims being made in both arguments and proposals. Both rhetorical modes, argumentation and proposing solutions to problems (problem solving) meet the classical definition of rhetoric that is designed to persuade, and that is both contain "a statement of a case and its proof."

Statistics.

Numbers can be convincing, and people are often swayed by data that can be quantified. To say that 70% of the population opposes a tax increase is an effective piece of reliable evidence, particularly if that total can be verified to your opponents' satisfaction. Statistics not only support your views through verifiable evidence, but they seem to suggest that you are not alone in advocating the positions that you do.

Appeals to Authority.

Being able to cite an expert lends a great deal of credence to your argument or proposal. If, for example, you advocate that corporations provide day care centers for the children of their employees, being able to cite leading authorities on child development as supporters of your viewpoint will certainly give more weight to your case. There is strength in numbers, and, if a number of well-qualified authorities support your position, you have a much greater chance of convincing your audience to your point of view.

Personal Testimonies.

Advertising attests to the power of personal testimonies to persuade. An advertisement for a new brand of cereal may include several persons speaking about how they have tasted the product and can verify that it has outstanding flavor and quality for the price. Political candidates bring forward all the time individual steel workers, farmers, teachers, computer technicians, and whatever other occupation might be helpful to testify that Joe Smith or Mary Jones is their candidate because no one else could better represent their interests. In your own writing, calling upon personal experiences you have been through, or calling upon the stories and testimonies of others, can be a very effective persuasive tool because it makes abstract issues seem more real and personal. Also, personal stories and testimonies create empathy in your audience and promote emotional responses, and you know from your study of previous chapters how effective a rhetorical tool for persuasion Aristotle considered *pathos*.

Factual Reference.

Factual references serve ends similar to statistics. They provide a verifiable, and at times irrefutable base of evidence upon which to construct an effective argument. If your facts are accurate, representative, and relevant to the point you wish to make, facts can be your strongest defense against an opponents attack upon your viewpoints.

Field Research.

Field research represents a type of observational visit. Most field research is based upon several visits to a specified site so that information can be gathered over time and in a range of settings. Generally, field research focuses upon the setting, the people involved, and the observer's personal reactions. The purpose of a field research report is to present a general impression of the site through the careful selection of details. Field research has great value to arguments and proposals that require a sense of a locale, an environment, a work setting, or a populace. Field research gives a degree of intimacy and immediacy to an argument by indicating that the researcher has visited the site or is using data based upon such first-hand observation.

Interviews.

Interviews allow a blending of a number of approaches central to proposals and argumentation. For one, they combine the intimacy and power of personal testimony with the scientific data appeal of statistics. In some instances, depending upon who is being interviewed, they allow for appeals to authority. Generally, they also combine some of the best qualities of field research in that the interviewer usually goes to the subject, rather than the person to be interviewed going to the interviewer. Interviews provide useful facts, data, details, and information and combine these factors with the intimacy of personal statements and reflections. They can be powerful persuasive tools for use as supporting examples in any argument or proposal.

Questionnaires.

Questionnaires represent interviews on a large scale. Generally, questionnaires are provided to a large group of respondents either on a random or a highly selective and defined basis. Questionnaires solicit opinions, so they are similar to interviews, and they also provide statistical data, so they take on the character of scientific empiricism. Since questionnaires can survey the opinions and attitudes of large numbers of people, they have the added impact of looking representative, as well as perhaps being important indicators of trends. Further, a great deal of validity is often attributed to questionnaires by audiences because questionnaires generally are designed to answer important questions about personal issues and societal problems.

Group Exercise #4

Each group will devise a proposition that can be investigated by some combination of the methods discussed above: statistics, appeals to authority, personal testimonies, factual references, field research, interviews, or questionnaires. The groups will then exchange their propositions with each other, and the second group will be responsible for structuring a problem solving approach to address the issues raised by the first group's proposition. The proposal for solving the problem, or responding to the issue, raised by the first group, will use several of the methods discussed above, as well as follow the model for structuring a problem solving paper presented in your textbook.

After this part of the exercise has been completed, the class will critique each group's proposal and offer suggestions for improvement, as well as for refinement or honing of techniques. The final phase of the exercise will involve the development of a general set of guidelines by the class on how to write effective problem solving papers.

Point/Counterpoint: Considering Opposing Arguments

1). A popular saying states that all solutions to problems only create new problems. Do you agree?

2). Your textbook states, "If the problem is solvable, however, the difficult part is to propose a solution and then persuade others that your solution will, in fact, solve the problem--without creating new problems and without costing too much." One question: if the problem is solvable, wouldn't that mean that a solution was already known? After all, how could you know a problem was solvable if you couldn't already conceptualize its solution? Your thoughts? Do you agree or disagree?

3). After a class on problem solving techniques, Shannon says to Terry, "I have a problem with this problem solving we are learning. If Aristotle says that *pathos* is the strongest of the verbal appeals, why am I bothering to study logic and to learn the techniques of well-reasoned arguments?"
What would your response be to Shannon's comment?

4). Continuing the conversation, Terry responds, "I think a bigger problem resides with *ethos*. If people are swayed by the character of a speaker or writer, what's to keep a clever and articulate person from assuming any *ethos* he or she thinks will work in a given situation? What's to keep anyone from assuming any guise or persona that gets the results he or she wants? Isn't there something strangely disturbing about this, maybe even unethical?"
How would you respond to Terry's views?

5). Analyze the following speech by Patrick Henry, American Revolutionary leader and orator, as an example of a problem solving proposal. Assess the speech in terms of Aristotle's views on *logos*, *pathos*, and *ethos*, as well as in terms of the model for writing problem solving essays presented to you by your text. Reflect upon what you decide and determine.

It is natural for man to indulge in the illusions of hope. We are apt to shut our eyes against a painful truth, and listen to that song of that siren till she transforms us into beasts. Is this the part of wide men, engaged in a great and arduous struggle for liberty? Are we disposed to be of the number of those, who, having eyes, see not, and having ears, hear not the things which so nearly concern their temporal salvation? For my part, whatever anguish of spirit it may cost, I am willing to know the whole truth; to know the worst, and to provide for it.
I have but one lamp by which my feet are guided; and that is the lamp of experience. I know of no way of judging of the future but by the past; and, judging by the past, I wish to know what there has been in the conduct of the British ministry

for the last ten years to justify those hopes with which gentlemen have been pleased to solace themselves and the house? Is it that insidious smile with which our petition has been lately received? Trust it not: it will prove a snare to your feet. Suffer not yourselves to be betrayed with a kiss. Ask yourselves, how this gracious reception of our petition comports with those warlike preparations which cover our waters and darken our land. Are fleets and armies necessary to a work of love and reconciliation? Have we shown ourselves so unwilling to be reconciled that force must be called in to win back our love? Let us not deceive ourselves. These are the implements of war and subjugation,--the last arguments to which kings resort.

I ask, gentlemen, what means this martial array, if its purpose be not to force us into submission? Can gentlemen assign any other possible motive for it? Has Great Britain any enemy in this quarter of the world, to call for all this accumulation of navies and armies? No, she has none. They are meant for us: they can be meant for no other. They are sent over to bind and rivet upon us those chains which the British ministry have been so long forging. And what have we to oppose to them? Shall we try argument? We hAve been trying that for the last ten years. Have we anything new to offer upon the subject? Nothing. We have held the subject up to every light in which it is capable; but it has been all in vain.

Shall we resort to entreaty and humble supplication? What terms shall we find which have not been already exhausted? Let us not, I beseech you, deceive ourselves longer. We have done everything that could be done, to avert the storm which is now coming on. We have petitioned; we have remonstrated; we have prostrated ourselves at the foot of the throne, and implored its interposition to arrest the tyrannical hands of the ministry and parliament. Our petitions have been slighted; our remonstrances have produced additional violence and insult; our supplications disregarded; and we have been spurned with contempt from the foot of the throne.

In vain, after these things, may we indulge the fond hope of peace and reconciliation. There is no longer any room for hope. If we wish to be free; if we mean to preserve inviolate those inestimable privileges for which we have been so long contending; if we mean not basely to abandon the noble struggle in which we have been so long engaged, and which we have pledged ourselves never to abandon until the glorious object of our contest shall be obtained--we must fight! I repeat it, we must fight! An appeal to arms and the God of Hosts, is all that is left us.

They tell us that we are weak; unable to cope with so formidable an adversary. But when shall we be stronger? Will it be the next week or the next year? Will it be when we are totally disarmed, and when a British guard shall be stationed in every house? Shall we gather strength by irresolution and inaction? Shall we acquire the means of effectual resistance by lying supinely on our backs, and hugging the delusive phantom of hope, until our enemies shall have bound us hand and foot? We are not weak, if we make a proper use of those means which the God of nature hath placed in our power.

Three millions of people, armed in the holy cause of liberty, and in such a country as that which we possess, are invincible by any force which our enemy can send against us. Besides, we shall not fight our battles alone. There is a just God who presides over the destinies of nations; and who will raise up friends to fight our battles for us. The battle is not to the strong alone; it is to the vigilant, the active, the brave. Besides, we have no election. If we were base enough to desire it, it is now too late to retire from the contest. There is no retreat but in submission and slavery! Our chains are forged. Their clanking may be heard on the plains of Boston! The war is inevitable; and let it come! I repeat it, let it come!

It is in vain to extenuate the matter. Gentlemen may cry peace, peace; but there is no peace. The war is actually begun. The next gale that sweeps from the north, will bring to our ears the clash of resounding arms! Our brethren are already in the field! Why stand we here idle? What is it that gentlemen wish? What would they have? Is life so dear, or peace so sweet, as to be purchased at the price of chains and slavery? Forbid it, Almighty God! I know not what course others may take; but as for me, give me liberty, or give me death.

6). A friend in your class has also done the analysis of Patrick Henry's speech in terms of the model for writing problem solving essays or proposals. She discovers that she thinks Henry's speech is an excellent example of a problem solving proposal, but it does not fit the model presented to her by the textbook. She has excellent and persuasive reasons for believing Henry's speech is an excellent example of a problem solving proposal, and she has a number of interesting critiques of the model for problem solving essays presented to her by the textbook. "It all comes down to this," she tells you. "Either Henry's speech is an excellent problem solving proposal and the model in the textbook is wrong or too limited, or the model in the textbook is correct and Henry's speech is a poor example of a problem solving proposal. Since I believe Henry's speech is excellent, I have no other choice but to believe that the model in my textbook is too limited."

How would you respond to your friend's comments?

7). Your friend Hank has a different response to the Patrick Henry assignment and to the model for problem solving essays presented in your textbook. "I'm frustrated," he says. "I can look at Henry's speech and know it's a great example of defining a problem and proposing a solution. I can look at the model in the text and see that it is a good one and an accurate description of how writing a problem solving essay could be done. But the problem is, what does any of this have to do with me? Just because I can understand the model in the text doesn't mean that I will automatically write well by following it. Just because I can see how well-written Henry's essay is doesn't mean I can write one like it. To me it's like listening to a recording of a great pianist playing Beethoven or some great musical genius like that and then being told, 'Okay, you've heard it; now you play it, too.' Just because you can recognize that something has been done well and can understand intellectually the process behind it, doesn't mean that you can do it, too. I think there's a fallacy in here somewhere, and definitely a problem."

How would you respond to Hank's concerns and objections?

SUMMARY AND ASSESSMENT PAGE

What ideas from *CHAPTER EIGHT: PROBLEM SOLVING* (in either your textbook or your workbook) helped you the most with your writing? What ideas or techniques did you hope to get from this chapter but did not? What steps do you intend to take to get those ideas or techniques?

"HAVE IDEAS THAT ARE CLEAR,

AND EXPRESSIONS THAT ARE SIMPLE"

--MME. DE CHARRIERE

CHAPTER NINE: ARGUING

Chapter Nine introduces you to a new rhetorical mode, that of argumentation or persuasion. Argumentation has an aim and purpose different from expressive writing and expository writing. In argumentation, the primary aim is neither to express the writer's feelings and identity (expressive writing) nor to explain a subject (expository writing) but to convince and persuade the reader to the writer's point of view. Since most writers direct their arguments toward readers who hold either a neutral or an opposing view from the writer's own, persuading the audience toward another point of view represents no small challenge.

The general structure of an argument is, as Aristotle indicated, "the statement of the case together with its proof." In persuasive writing, the "statement of the case" is called the *proposition*, or the thesis, and the proof is called the *evidence*. All arguments present a thesis or proposition to be argued, together with the evidence that will support that proposition and defend it against challenges from opposing viewpoints. The proposition or thesis of an argument must be for or against something. It cannot take a neutral stance, and it should not straddle the fence.

The moment a proposition is framed for an argument, a rudimentary sense of organization is also suggested. To argue for the correctness of viewpoint X and to convince an audience who thought otherwise, you would have to: (1) muster sufficient evidence to back up your views and to withstand challenges from the opposition; and (2) anticipate the objections the opposition might raise so that you could counter them at some point in your essay.

This two-point strategy represents a simplification of the classical argument form. In classical rhetoric, argumentation, or formal persuasion, involved:

* An introduction (*Exordium*) in which the writer endeavors to capture the reader's attention and to establish some type of intellectual rapport with the audience.

* A statement of necessary background information (*Narratio*) relevant to the issue to be argued.

* An exposition (*Explicatio*) or definition (*Definitio*) of terms and issues involved in the argument.

* A statement of the proposition to be argued (*Partitio*).

* A presentation of the forms of evidence to substantiate the proposition (*Amplificatio*).

* A refutation of opposing arguments (*Refutatio*).

* A conclusion (*Peroratio* or *Epilogus*), in which the writer makes a strong final appeal to the audience for agreement, action, or change.

In persuasive writing, the abilities to reason well and to use language effectively are the writer's most important tools. Since, in persuasive writing, the emphasis is upon the audience, it is important early in the argument to establish rapport with the audience and to show a fair-minded, intellectual respect for the audience's views, as well as for the views of your opponents or challengers. Writers who start from the assumption that anyone who does not think as they do deserves to be castigated and rebuked will not get very far in persuading an audience to adopt a different perspective upon an issue. Writers who respect differences of opinion but all the while use rhetorical techniques to persuade and convince the audience to look at an issue from another perspective will be much more successful in their aims than writers who operate from a position of attack and condemnation.

Of equal importance is that you seek to establish early with your audience your own credibility. Your credibility with the audience and the rapport you establish are both part of your *ethos*. You must establish yourself as someone knowledgeable about your subject, fair-minded in considering and respecting a number of viewpoints, sincere, but non-judgmental in your efforts to convince and persuade, sensitive to your audience's frame of reference, aware of the voice or *ethos* you need to project with your audience, and aware of how much knowledge your audience needs to have about your subject. All of these issues are issues of rhetorical technique, and the person who masters these techniques will be a more persuasive arguer than the person who is unaware of the requirements of audience analysis and of argumentation as a rhetorical form.

The two most common modes of reasoning in argumentation are *inductive reasoning* and *deductive reasoning*. Inductive reasoning moves from evidence to a general conclusion, while deductive reasoning moves from a general assumption to a specific conclusion. Most arguments represent a blend of these two modes as writers seek to make their case for positions they assume to be correct.

Deductive reasoning has the longer heritage and comes to us from the classical era. Aristotle introduced the concept of deductive reasoning with the *syllogism*, a form of deductive reasoning that involves a major premise, a minor premise, and a conclusion. There are three general types of syllogisms, *categorical*, *disjunctive*, and *hypothetical*.

The categorical syllogism has to do with categories or whole classes and operates on the assumption that what is true for a class as a whole will also be true of its members.

All men are mortal.

John Smith is a man.

Therefore John Smith is mortal.

If all the statements in a syllogism are phrased in the positive, the conclusion will also be positive. If one premise is in the negative, the conclusion will also be in the negative.

No men are mortal

John Smith is a man.

Therefore John Smith is not mortal.

A syllogism with two negative premises generally yields no logical conclusion.

No men are mortal.

John Smith is not a man.

No logical conclusion possible.

Often in ordinary conversation syllogistic reasoning appears in an abbreviated form known as an *enthymeme*, in which one of the premises is stated and one is implied. For example, "Susan is an excellent chess player. She'd probably be good at bridge, too." In this enthymeme, the hidden premise is that people who are good at chess are also good at bridge; you can see, too, that there is an effort to define a class: all people good at chess are also good at bridge. Susan is assumed to be one example of this class.

The disjunctive syllogism deals with contraries and contradictions. Two alternatives (or contraries) are presented in the major premise, and the minor premise eliminates one of them.

Susan is either unkind or misinformed.

Susan is not unkind.

Therefore Susan is misinformed.

This disjunctive syllogism will only work if the two terms remain constant. We could not say, for example, "Susan is either unkind or misinformed./ Susan is not unkind./ Therefore, Susan is incompetent." This would not be a logical conclusion that could be drawn from these two premises.

The hypothetical syllogism is closely related to issues of cause and effect. An easy way to think of this type of syllogism is that it affirms or denies an *if/then* line of reasoning.

If social workers are not adequately paid, the quality of social service care will decline.

Social workers are not adequately paid.

Therefore the quality of social service care will decline.

The reasoning structure opposite to deduction is induction, in which a general assumption or statement is made about a class based upon an examination of a number of samples within that class. The movement of the line of reasoning is from particular to general, while, in deductive reasoning, the line of thought is from general to specific.

Inductive reasoning is generally the type of reasoning we use, often unconsciously, to form our world views. If we have a happy childhood in which we are treated lovingly and with care, if we move into our adolescence with good, caring friends, and if we fall in love in our adult years and have that love returned, we are likely to conclude, based on inductive reasoning, that people are good at heart and worth trusting. If, however, we have a difficult childhood in which we have trouble getting our needs met, our efforts to make friends as a child and adolescent are unsuccessful and frustrating, and our love is not returned as an adult, we are likely to conclude that the world is an unsafe place and people are not to be trusted. Unfortunately, inductive reasoning is also at the core of much of our prejudiced thinking and our capacity to develop stereotypes. If our experience of green-eyed people is that they were not kind people, we are likely to conclude through inductive reasoning that all green-eyed people are unkind.

Two types of inductive reasoning generally are distinguished, *perfect induction* and *scientific induction*. Perfect induction, in which all the members of a class are examined in relation to a particular trait, is the more rare. One could, for example, draw accurate conclusions as a whole about the physical endurance capabilities of men who entered the Navy during 1965-1985 after an examination of the records of each individual.

Scientific induction, on the other hand, allows for representative sampling and is, by far, the more common use to which inductive reasoning is put. Polling, questionnaires, interviews, field research all can yield valid information if: (1) the number of samples examined is large; (2) the samples are representative; and (3) allowance is made for atypical samples, or exceptions to the rule (or generalization). Since all inductive reasoning moves from evidence to a conclusion, it is important that the quality of the evidence is high and that the evidence itself is representative and not slanted or biased.

Errors in reasoning, known as *fallacies*, can be made when individuals are using either deductive or inductive reasoning. Some of the more common fallacies include:

Ad hoc, in which because X and Y occur together X is assumed to have caused Y. "I played my best round of golf wearing a plaid shirt; I'm going to wear a plaid shirt the next time I play." In our everyday lives, much of the power attributed to "lucky charms" is the result of *ad hoc* reasoning. Just because a student performed well on a biology exam while he was carrying a rabbit's foot in his pocket is no guarantee that the rabbit's foot had anything to do with the student's good grade.

Ad hominem, in which the character of the speaker, rather than the quality of his or her argument, is attacked. "Don't listen to John's views on economics; he's a Socialist."

Ad populem, in which an argument is formulated upon an appeal to popular prejudices and biases. "Don't listen to John's views on family life; he's a homosexual."

The Bandwagon, which assumes that something is correct because "everybody" is doing it. "Sensatia sunglasses are excellent; everybody's wearing them."

Begging the question, in which an assumption is taken for granted that needs to be established by proof. "Don't trust John on investments; he's a liar"--rather than establishing that John is lying in this particular instance.

Circular argument, in which a statement simply restates rather than proves its claim. "Women make wonderful mothers because they have motherly instincts."

Either/Or, a fallacy in which a complex issue is reduced to only two alternatives. "Either we eliminate drug use in our high schools or American education is doomed."

False analogy, in which there are not enough important similarities between two

169

subjects being compared to warrant the conclusions being drawn. "Political radicals are just like psycopaths; they both think the system is unjust and unfair."

False cause, a simplifying and reductivist form of reasoning in which a complex issue that is the result of many causes is explained in terms of only one cause. "The decline of the American family can be attributed directly to the Women's Liberation movement."

Genetic fallacy, in which the class that a person is from, and not the person's own qualities or qualifications, becomes the standard of judgment. "You can't possibly trust Howard; he's a lawyer."

Hasty generalization [Insufficient sampling], in which the sample is too small for logical conclusions to be drawn. "All athletes are bad in math; my friends, Joe and Carol, are on the swim team, and they can't even pass algebra."

Hidden generalization, in which one premise is left out or excluded from the argument in a fashion similar to an enthymeme. "Bob graduated from Harvard, so his family must have political connections." The hidden assumption or premise here is that all people who graduate from Harvard come from families of wealth and political power.

Insufficient sampling, in which the sample is too small for logical conclusions to be drawn. "Seafood restaurants are no good; I got sick in one the other night."

Post hoc, the type of faulty reasoning that assumes that, because one thing follows another, the second has been caused by the first. Scientific experiments are good at revealing the type of incorrect conclusions that can be drawn from *post hoc* reasoning. In one experiment, rats are fed early in the morning a sample of food X that is contaminated and that will make them ill within three hours. Two and a half hours later (and just before they are to become ill from food sample X), the rats are fed a perfectly fine, uncontaminated sample of food Y. When the rats become ill a few minutes later, it is food Y they will avoid from that point on, and not food X.

Red Herring, in which the audience is diverted from the real issue. Urged to install pollution controls in its factories, a company might argue that the increased cost of the pollution controls will necessitate job layoffs, a result that nobody would want. Instead of focusing upon the issue of pollution control, the company will use the red herring of job layoffs to divert attention from the real issue.

Rigged question, a fallacy that poses a question in such a way that any answer requires an admission of guilt. "Have you stopped cheating on your income taxes?" "Yes" implies that I have cheated, and "No" implies that I am still cheating on my taxes. There is no way for me to respond that is not destructive and incriminating.

Slanting, a fallacy in which language or data are represented in terms to encourage the reader to take a different or slanted view of the subject. To argue, for example, that the fact that 30% of all marriages fail is proof that marriage is a declining societal institution overlooks the fact that 70% of all marriages do not fail.

Sliding slope, in which one aspect of an argument is pushed to an extreme and illogical conclusion. "If a person smokes marijuana, the next step is cocaine, then heroin, then the total collapse of that person's moral character."

Unrepresentative sample, in which the samples used are not representative of the whole group. "92% of all women surveyed oppose abortion" is an unrepresentative sample if the only women surveyed were members of a fundamentalist religious group.

In addition to logical fallacies, there are also a number of psychological fallacies that play upon the feelings of the audience. Both *ad hominem* and *ad populem* fallacies belong to this category.

Rhetoric recognizes the legitimate role of *pathos*, or a sensitivity to the feelings of the audience, but psychological fallacies, however, cloud issues with extraneous material and divert the audience's attention from important issues at hand. Other examples of psychological fallacies include:

Appeal to pity, in which an extraneous appeal is used to draw unwarranted pity and sympathy from an audience. "I shouldn't have to fail my math class; my dog was sick at the time I took the test."

Appeal to force, in which one's social, political, or economic power over an individual gives more weight to one's argument or line of reasoning. "Don's proposal for a merger of our company with Holcraft Industries is an excellent one; if you don't vote for it, I won't promote you to assistant manager and you might lose you job entirely."

Appeal to ceremony, in which the locale and formality are assumed to give truth and importance to data and/or conclusions. When TV ads present information on the latest cold medicines, the odds are that the speaker in the ad will be wearing a white lab coat and/or standing in front of a nurse's or doctor's station on a hospital floor. The presence of such props lends a type of false credence to the information the speaker is presenting. The cold medicine will be good or bad, and the test results will substantiate or negate this fact, whether the spokesperson is dressed in a white lab coat or not or speaks to you from any number of locales or settings.

Appeal to tradition, assumes that because something has always been done a certain way (or done a certain way for a long period of time) that that way of doing things has intrinsic merit and is *a priori* better than other methods that might be proposed. "We cannot change to an automated system of registration; we've been registering students for their classes without data processing for over eighty years, and there's no need to change the system now."

Appeal to ignorance, which assumes that a proposition that cannot be proven false must be true. "No one can prove that God doesn't exist, so God must exist."

Appeal to humor, in which humor is used to denigrate an opponent or trivialize his or her views. "We all know why Congresswoman Blake is opposed to an economic ban on South Africa; South Africa is a leading exporter of diamonds, and we all know how women love their diamonds."

Group Exercise #1

The class is to divide into groups, and each group is to design an advertising campaign, a political campaign, or a political action movement that uses a substantial number of the logical fallacies or psychological fallacies in its appeals. After each group has presented its ideas, the class will discuss the rhetorical strategies used by each group and evaluate the types of impact such strategies might have upon an audience.

In a variant of this idea, individuals or groups can bring to class examples from the print media of essays, ads, campaign literature, speeches, bumper stickers, etc., in which logical fallacies or psychological fallacies play a large role in influencing audience response. Examples from the visual media, such as TV ads and billboards, can be discussed in this context, too.

The structuring of argumentation essays depends upon a series of statements connected by logical appeals. An argument can be constructed around any debatable topic, but it helps if you have an interest in the subject and care about its implications. Like all essays, argumentation essays work best if the topic has been narrowed. "Banning smoking," for example, is far too wide a topic to be handled successfully, but "banning smoking in public facilities" offers a more manageable format.

The nature of argumentation essays requires that you define your terms and gather appropriate supporting evidence. Never assume that any term shares the same meaning for your audience, even a term in common usage, like *love*. Use evidence wisely and be sure that you are interpreting it fairly and consistently. When drawing upon factual evidence, be sure that you are quoting accurately and not taking a quotation out of context in such a way that you distort its meaning. If, for example, you read a book review by Morgan Terry that states "I have severe doubts that *The Face of Morning* is an American masterpiece of high literary quality," and you quote Terry as saying "*The Face of Morning* is an American masterpiece of high literary quality," you have distorted the content and the intent of Terry's review. Often ellipses (. . .) are used to indicate that portions of a statement have been left out, but even a phrasing like, "*The Face of Morning* '. . . is an American masterpiece of high literary quality,' says Morgan Terry,'" is a distortion of the idea of the original review.

A substantial number of argumentation essays you will write will depend upon your interpretation of statements, data, or case studies, or quotations from noted authorities in a field. Your ability to interpret and evaluate will be extremely important to drawing the meaning from the material, formulating a proposition, and structuring your proofs to defend your position. Certainly, for a number of argumentation essays, you will be encouraged to research your facts before presenting your case, but, in a number of instances, particularly in taking essay examinations in college and graduate school, you will be presented with material to interpret and evaluate without the assistance of outside reference sources. You will be called upon to interpret, state a position, and defend that position using your best logical and rhetorical skills.

Exercise #1

Exercise #1 provides you an opportunity to interpret a passage, state a proposition or thesis, and defend your thesis through logical reasoning. The process itself is similar to taking an essay examination in that the interpretation of this passage depends more upon your critical thinking skills and rhetorical resources than it does upon heavily researched evidence. Read the passage and make your best case for whatever point of view you adopt.

Here is a very familiar parable, the parable of the prodigal son (Luke 15: 11-32):

A man had two sons. When the younger told his father, "I want my share of your estate now, instead of waiting until you die!" his father agreed to divide his wealth between his sons.

A few days later this younger son packed all his belongings and took a trip to a distant land, and there wasted all his money on parties and prostitutes. About the time his money was gone a great famine swept over the land, and he began to starve.

He persuaded a local farmer to hire him to feed his pigs. The boy became so hungry that even the pods he was feeding the swine looked good to him. And no one gave him anything.

When he finally came to his senses, he said to himself, "At home even the hired men have food enough and to spare, and here I am dying of hunger! I will go home to my father and say, "Father, I have sinned against both heaven and you, and am no longer worthy of being called your son. Please take me on as a hired man."

So he returned home to his father. And while he was still a long distance away, his father saw him coming and was filled with loving pity and ran and embraced him and kissed him.

His son said to him, "Father I have sinned against heaven and you, and am not worthy of being called your son."

But his father said to the slaves, "Quick! Bring the finest robe in the house and put it on him. And a jeweled ring for his finger; and shoes. And kill the calf we have in the fattening pen. We must celebrate with a feast, for this son of mine was dead and has returned to life. He was lost and is found." So the party began.

Meanwhile, the older son was in the fields working; when he returned home, he heard dance music coming from the house, and he asked one of the servants what was going on.

"Your brother is back," he was told, "and your father has killed the calf we were fattening and has prepared a great feast to celebrate his coming home again unharmed."

The older brother was angry and wouldn't go in. His father came out and begged him, but he replied, "All these years I've worked hard for you and never once refused to do a single thing you told me to; and in all that time you never gave me even one young goat for a feast with my friends. Yet when this son of yours comes back after spending your money on prostitutes, you celebrate by killing the finest calf we have on the place.

"Look, dear son," his father said to him, "you and I are very close, and everything I have is yours. But it is right to celebrate. For he is your brother; and he was dead and has come back to life! He was lost and is found!"

Your assignment for this exercise is to address this question: Does the older brother have a case? Can a good argument be made for the feelings and the viewpoint he expresses?

You will probably be able to intuit rather quickly that most arguments afford you one of three positions to defend: yes (the affirmative), no (the negative), or a qualified yes/no (a compromise, mid-position that allows for yes or no under limited and carefully spelled out conditions. For example, on the issue of whether abortion should remain legalized in America, one could argue *yes* under all circumstances; *no* under all circumstances; or a *qualified yes/no*, in which abortions would be opposed, in general, but exceptions would be made for situations of rape, incest, fetal deformity, and threats to the health of the mother.

Exercise #2

Return to the parable of the prodigal son and formulate propositions (thesis statements) for arguments that would be responding to the issue of whether the elder son had a case by answering yes in the affirmative, no in the negative, or a qualified yes/no with a specified set of circumstances that defined how broadly the yes or no would be applied. Develop one thesis statement, or proposition, for each of these viewpoints.

Free Writing #1

Interpreting what you think is the central concern of the parable of the prodigal son (such as love, forgiveness, etc.) is a preliminary stage to addressing the issue of whether a case can be made for the elder son's position. Discuss what you consider to be the central concern of the parable and how your interpretation influenced the argument you developed.

Exercise #3

Consider the following passage, which is an abstract of an essay on feminist theories of literacy. Interpret what you think is the main idea (or thesis) of the passage and evaluate the thesis's validity. Formulate a response of your own to the ideas presented in the passage. Do you agree, disagree, agree in some instances but not in others? Write your response out as if it were a thesis statement for an argumentation essay.

Toward a Feminist Definition of Literacy

As feminism emerges as a central topic for critical inquiry within academe, an interesting irony has developed. Feminism itself is very often a challenge to the types of philosophical assumptions that underlie academic knowledge and a reaction to the codifications of linear thinking generally associated with traditional Aristotelian modes of cognition. Yet it is these Aristotelian modes themselves that generally define and determine what constitutes literacy in our culture. Linear and dichotomized modes of cognition, together with traditional models of discourse that favor non-reflexive expression over reflexive, are the main avenues by which we define and assess literacy in our culture today--yet these are the very modes that minimize feminist ways of knowing and being in contemporary culture. To define literacy fully and fairly is to seek a philosophical stance inclusive of the epistemological bases of feminism and open to more non-traditional methods of cognition and expression than the typical subject/object dichotomies of logocentric Aristotelian dualism.

Exercise #4

Interpreting and drawing inferences from printed sources are important critical thinking skills, especially for the process of argumentation and persuasion. Do you agree? Why or why not?

Exercise #5

Apply your skills in interpretation to the following passage, which is a Chinese parable. What inferences can be drawn from this parable? How can those inferences be formulated into propositional thesis statements for argumentation essays?

On a certain street in a Chinese city there was a poor beggar who held out his cup all day begging for rice or whatever the passers-by chose to give him.

One day the beggar say a great parade coming down his street headed by the

Emperor riding in his stately rickshaw and freely handing out gifts to his subjects. The poor beggar was filled with delight.

"Now," thought Woo, "my great opportunity has come. For once I shall receive a worthy gift," and he danced with joy.

When the Emperor reached him, Woo held out his cup with great earnestness, but instead of the expected gift from the Emperor his majesty asked Woo for a gift.

Poor Woo was greatly disappointed and vexed; so he reached in his cup and with much grumbling handed the Emperor two of the smallest grains of rice he could find. The Emperor passed on.

All that day Woo was fumed and grumbled. He denounced the Emperor, he berated Buddha, he was cross to those who spoke to him, and few people even stopped to speak to him or drop grains of rice in his cup.

That night when Woo reached his poor hut and poured out his scant supply of rice, he found in his cup two nuggets of gold just the size of the grains of rice he had given to the Emperor.

Exercise #6

Following the line of reasoning in Exercise #5, what inferences can be drawn from the following passage and formulated into propositional statements (thesis statements) for argumentation essays?

Thomas Aquinas (1225-1274) was a famous philosopher during the medieval period. When Aquinas was a young boy, about six years of age, he was not very well-liked by his schoolmates because he was very quiet and withdrawn. One day, his schoolmates decided to tease Aquinas by playing a practical joke on him.

"Aquinas," come quickly," one of them shouted. "There's a blue ox flying by the window!"

Aquinas ran immediately to the window and looked out, and his schoolmates fell on the floor with laughter at what they thought was his stupidity.

"How could you be so stupid," one of them asked Aquinas, "as to think that a blue ox could fly?"

Aquinas replied, "I'd rather believe that a blue ox could fly, than to think that my friends would lie to me."

The story of Aquinas and his schoolmates offers many possible interpretations about human nature and why people do what they do. Discuss what aspect of this story stands out for you the most as a commentary on human nature.

Exercise #7

Again, following along the lines of Exercises #5 and #6, interpret the following passage and draw from it propositional statements (thesis statements) around which you could structure an argumentation essay.

Former President Jimmy Carter tells the following story:

When Carter was a lieutenant in the Navy, he was selected to interview for the position of aide to an admiral. All went well with the interview, according to Carter, with the admiral asking the usual questions about Carter's background, training, and career aspirations. Then the admiral looked at Carter and said, "Mr. Carter, I wish to ask you one last question, and the most important question in my eyes: Have you always tried to do your best?"

Carter says he thought for a moment and then replied to the admiral, "No, sir. I can't say that I have always tried to do my best."

"Why not, Mr. Carter?" the admiral said. "Why not?"

Jimmy Carter says that this episode with the Admiral had a profound effect upon him by forcing Carter not only to realize that he had not always tried to do his best, but that he had to try to search his soul and conscience for reasons to explain why. Carter says this incident stayed with him for the rest of his life and became a turning point in his own understanding and assessment of himself.

Free Writing #3

What do you think of this episode? What do you think it is that keeps people from always trying to do their best? Have you always tried to do your best? If not, why not?

An important part of writing effective argumentation essays is refuting counterarguments, or arguments offered against your own. Addressing counterarguments gives weight and merit to argumentation essays by indicating that the author has carefully thought out the implications of his or her views. If handled diplomatically, addressing counterarguments can often influence the views and beliefs of your audience.

The tone of your refutation is an all-important factor. With the right tone, you will convince; with too strident or defensive a tone, you will turn off your audience and perhaps even lose points that you have gained previously. Strive to create the tone of an informed and open-minded debater who is considering issues from a number of angles. Seem reasonable, but not pompous or arrogant; assertive, but not overbearing. Above all, do not ridicule your opposition or engage in name calling or personal attacks.

In refuting counterarguments, you have the options of (1) pointing out their logical weaknesses; (2) indicating possible disadvantages if these ideas are accepted or implemented; (3) questioning the nature and validity of your opponents' evidence; (4) questioning the practicality of the approach suggested by the counterarguments; and (5) presenting new data that calls into question the strength of your opponent's position. Any or all of these strategies used with skill and with an analytical tone that avoids being vituperative can be very powerful tools for diminishing the impact of your opponents' views and "re-persuading" your audience to the truth of your position.

Group Exercise #2

Have the class focus upon any essay presented in the textbook, or bring to class sample essays, and set about the process of (1) determining what are the main claims or central ideas of each essay; and (2) developing counterarguments to refute the positions developed in each sample essay.

As an additional aspect of this exercise, have the class try presenting counterarguments by using the techniques of Rogerian argument.

Point/Counterpoint: Considering Opposing Arguments

1. The first Free Writing presented to you in Chapter Nine of your textbook is to argue either for or against the following claim: "High schools today are a waste of time." Argue for or against the claim that this *topic* is a waste of time.

2. Consider the Rogerian model for argumentation, which holds that persuasion is more likely to occur in a friendly environment than in an antagonistic one. Do you agree with this viewpoint, or do you feel that it is naive, perhaps even possibly misguided? Can you think of situations in which such an empathetic view of one's opposition could work against the success of the point one was making with an audience?

3. What reasons could you think of for using a Rogerian strategy for argumentation versus other approaches? Do you feel the Rogerian approach will be more successful with groups who have a similarity of viewpoint than with groups compromised of polar ideas and attitudes? Why might that be?

4. Two assumptions underlie most views of argumentation: (1) that a reasoned, intellectual approach is the best (or at least preferred) method to take and is the most effective in winning over an audience; and (2) that the majority of (if not all) arguments can be solved or resolved through reasoned discourse and an exchange of ideas that then become open to scrutiny and question. Do you agree with these assumptions? Why or why not? Are there other assumptions you would propose as more valid? What might those be?

5. Another model for argumentation not discussed in full detail in your textbook is the Toulmin model, developed by Stephen Toulmin, a rhetorician and logician. Research the Toulmin model and (1) argue for or against its validity as a model of argumentation; (2) discuss what value the Toulmin model might have to your own argumentation strategies; and (3) compare and contrast the Toulmin model with the Rogerian and the classical models of argumentation.

6. A fellow classmate tells you that the study of argumentation has given him great hope. Opposing viewpoints can be presented, discussed, and reconciled, and, in this way, truth can be arrived at. What would be your response to your classmate? Do you agree with his views? Do you think truth can be arrived at via argumentation? What would be your definition of truth in terms of argumentation? How would an audience know when and how that truth had been arrived at?

SUMMARY AND ASSESSMENT PAGE

What ideas from *CHAPTER NINE: ARGUING* (in either your textbook or your workbook) helped you the most with your writing? What ideas or techniques did you hope to get from this chapter but did not? What steps do you intend to take to learn those ideas or techniques?

"CHANGE AND GROWTH TAKE PLACE WHEN A PERSON HAS RISKED HIMSELF AND DARES TO BECOME INVOLVED WITH EXPERIMENTING WITH HIS OWN LIFE."

--HERBERT OTTO

CHAPTER TEN: EXPLORING

Free Writing #1

Your textbook states that "most writing begins with a sense of exploration." Do you agree?

What do the terms *explore* and *discover* mean to you?

Free Writing #3

Journal entries; free writings; essays; workbook exercises. Which of these writing forms has/have been the most helpful to you in helping you explore your own ideas?

Free Writing #4

Which of the writing forms has/have been most helpful to you in helping you discover/explore your ideas as a writer?

Free Writing #5

What do you think Herbert Otto means when he says, "Change and growth take place when a person has risked himself and dares to become involved with experimenting with his own life?"

Explore, from the Latin *explorare*, meaning "to search out." Explore: to systematically investigate; examine; to study.

Exercise #1

What is the difference, in your mind, between the type of writing required for observing, describing, remembering, and the type required for exploring?

Exercise #2

Your textbook states that "exploratory essays often border on argumentation, but in the end they do not take sides or advocate any one position." Do you agree or disagree?

Exercise #3

Your textbook states that "the writer's specific, personal experience is central to all exploratory writing." Do you agree or disagree?

Free Writing #6

Discuss/Describe how "the writer's specific, personal experience" has been central to your exploratory writing.

Group Exercise #1

Consider the two essays, "On Conversation" by Andy Rooney and "The Fate of the Dinosaur" by Ellen Goodman, presented in your textbook. Discuss the similarities and the differences in these two works as examples of exploratory writing. From your discussions, describe what might be some important characteristics of a well-written exploratory essay.

Exercise #4

Discuss/Describe a personal experience similar to the ones related by Rooney and Goodman that might serve as the topic of an exploratory essay. Do you feel more exploratory essays develop out of adults reflecting upon childhood and youth or adult reflecting upon adult experiences? Why do you think that might be?

Exercise #5

Compare Loren Eiseley's essay, "The Bird and the Machine," with the essays by Rooney and Goodman. Eiseley's essay is more metaphysical in scope, using a personal experience to reflect upon the mysteries of the universe, while Rooney's and Goodman's focus upon the insight to be found in the experience itself and its relationship to their lives as a whole.

Discuss what you see are differences in approach, organization, and style between Eiseley's essay and Rooney's and Goodman's. Do you think any generalizations can be drawn from your exploration about the nature of the exploratory essay that is metaphysical in scope?

Free Writing #7

Eiseley's essay describes a change of mind and a change of heart. Have you ever had a similar experience, one in which you were going about your business, convinced that you were doing what you were supposed to do, and then something happened to cause you to rethink your values?

The concept of exploration can be divided into two aspects, *formal exploration* and *informal exploration*. *Formal exploration* is the type associated with researching a topic and generally involves some type of library or field research. *Informal exploration* has more to do with thinking something through on one's own; often another term for informal exploration is a *speculation, meditation,* or *reflection*. People often reflect upon their lives, or upon a topic of interest to them, and this type of writing is considered a type of speculation or meditation upon a subject. Some of the best personal voice essays are speculative, informal explorations, and this genre of writing has a long and respected tradition.

As you will note with Eiseley's essay, memory often plays a large part in an informal exploration, as do feelings and a desire to interpret the experience recalled from a new, and often wiser, perspective. Often the tone of the informal exploratory essay is determined by the nature of the perspective the writer has obtained between the original event and his or her "looking back over" the event from the perspective of time gone by.

If the event triggers pleasant feelings and memories, the tone of the essay is very warm and engaging, almost nostalgic. Certainly, Maya Angelou's essay would qualify as a type of pleasant, nostalgic, informal exploration of her feelings associated with Stamps, Arkansas and with her grandmother's store.

If the event brings back sad or even unpleasant associations, the tone of the essay can be much more somber. Such an element pervades Eiseley's essay, for certainly there is a sense of his regret at caging the bird and his early, youthful insensitivity to the life energy of animals. What took precedence in his mind at the time was performing his job; the bird was only one small detail to handle, not a living entity that deserved his respect and compassion. This mood or tone of the essay splits, however, into one of joy and of great empathetic respect for the two birds and for the lesson they taught Eiseley about love, hope, freedom, and the ultimate difference between living beings and machines. At this point, the essay explores Eiseley's sense of wonder at the created world and how no machine will ever duplicate feelings of love, hope, compassion, and empathy.

Group Exercise #2

Psychologist Carl Rogers has stated, "The only man who is educated is the man who has learned to learn; the man who has learned how to adapt and change; the man who has realized that no knowledge is secure, that only the process of seeking knowledge gives a basis for security."

Have the class divide into groups and discuss the significance of this quotation. Is there agreement with Rogers' views? What definitions of *knowledge* and *learning* is Rogers proposing? Do Rogers' views of knowledge and learning relate to Eiseley's essay? How? In what way? If not, why not?

Informal explorations call upon many critical thinking skills, especially the ability to observe, recall, ponder, infer, intuit, and assess. In addition, informal exploratory essays call upon one more skill that some expository essays do not, and that is a strong dimension of personal voice. Some expository essays that explain and develop information do not depend upon a strong personal voice to communicate their ideas, but informal exploratory essays almost always do. Thus, the form requires that the writer be, to a degree, self-revealing and self-disclosing.

These factors make the informal exploratory essay more difficult for some writers, but they should not be thought of as insurmountable barriers largely because a fact of the writing process is that people find ways to express what matters to them to express. Remember Russell Baker's essay on the art of eating spaghetti. That became a self-revealing essay with strong personal voice because the idea of writing about memories of his family inspired Baker to open up and explore his memories and his feelings. The result was an essay that was moving, speculative, and reflective--rather than an objective, expository description.

Often this is the greatest value of informal exploratory essays--they open up to us memories, thoughts, feelings, perspectives, and insights of which we are unaware. Once this treasure house of memories (as Quintilian phrased it) is affected, opened up by emotion and recollection, the power to write movingly and persuasively is also opened up and freed.

Exercise #6

One advantage attributed to informal exploratory writing is that it enables us to tap into the "inner voices" in our consciousness that carry a great many of our memories, emotions, attitudes, longings, and dreams. Do you agree with this view? If so, what "inner voices" do you reach through informal exploratory writing? What benefit do you feel you derive from this process to further your own writing skills? If you disagree, explain why and offer an alternative model or explanation.

Free Writing #8

Free write an informal exploratory essay on one of the following topics. Remember that the key word here is *explore*.

* affection

* trust

* wit

* kindness

* humor

* nervousness

* innocence

* merit

* safety

* tenderness

* contentment

Exercise #7

Do the terms *investigate* and *explore* have different meanings for you? What would be the difference or distinction between the two? If you feel they are the same or very similar, explain why you think so.

By virtue of the fact that you are human, you are a learner. As you know from Chapter Eight, Aristotle believed that "all men by nature desire to learn." A great deal of why the informal exploratory essay form has survived for as long as it has and has produced so many masterpieces of insight is its capacity to stir a person's desire to learn.

One area in particular stands out, and that is the desire to learn more about oneself. Often the term *inventory* is used here to indicate a type of "taking stock" and seeing who we have been and who we are on the road to becoming. Exploring our learning processes enables us to discover, too, potentials for creativity and insight that we might not have known we possessed.

Exercise #8

Observe your actions and record the objective facts of your behavior. Keep notes like this on yourself for about one week; at the end of the week, use your information as a data base from which you can draw for a writing assignment based upon this topic.

Exercise #9

The following are some of the characteristics generally identified with a good learner.

* *Purposeful*

* *Motivated*

* *Good Control of Anxiety*

* *Self-disciplined*

* *Creative*

* *Resourceful*

* *Independent Thinker*

* *Planner*

* *Well-Organized*

* *Inquisitive*

* *Speculative and Philosophical*

Using these concepts as your guide, explore your skills and interests as a learner. Do you fit the model? Do you agree with the model? If not, what concepts would you change, what new ones would you include?

One aspect of exploring is your ability to use your mind's mental pictures as departure points for your thoughts. The mind thinks in visual imagery, and some theorists tell us that an ability to use the mind's capacity for mental imagery is central to the creative process. In exploring your ideas, rely upon the images, memories, and fantasies your mind can generate. Your unconscious mind is a rich repository of ideas, and mental imagery enables you to tap this resource and use it to your advantage in your writing. Awareness is the key. Become aware of your mind's thinking processes, and focus upon the images that appear in your mind and that deserve exploration. Mental images, like ideas, will pop into your mind at unusual and unexpected times--not always on the schedule you might have hoped for--and a key to expanding your awareness and your creative potential is to respect the ideas that have surfaced and to allow them expression.

Many writers carry a small notebook around in which they record their thoughts. Jotting down ideas as they come to you is an invaluable resource, a record of your mind interacting with life experiences. Jotting down ideas not only gives you ideas and material for future writing assignments, but it enables you to become increasingly more aware of your surroundings and of your inner mental voices and pictures.

One technique that might help you envision the importance of mental imagery to your writing is to think of your life as if it were a movie. This sounds like a strange concept, but thinking about your life in this way enables you to sense that your life is not static or linear, but dynamic and organic. So, too, is your creativity, as the concept of the "stream of consciousness" (discussed in earlier chapters) suggests.

Free Writing #9

If your life is a movie, what are its themes? What ideas play throughout your mind and indicate to you issues/ideas/feelings you might want to explore?

If you do not think of your life as a movie, what concept or analogy would you use to best describe it? Why this choice versus others you might have made?

Despite the fact that many individuals might view exploration as self-indulgent and frivolous, choosing, instead, to direct their energies outward, the concept of exploration remains a valuable intellectual tool for investigating the self and one's experiences. The power of exploration is that it allows for self-insight, which is at the heart of much important and excellent writing, be it expository, expressive, or exploratory in nature.

Point/Counterpoint: Considering Opposing Arguments

1. "Exploration seems, to me, self-indulgent," Jason says. "I am more interested in writing that will advance my career, like technical writing and journalism. Why do we have to do this, anyway?"

How would you respond to Jason?

2. Paula listens to Jason and replies, "I'm not opposed to exploratory writing because I think the idea of knowing more about yourself is a good one. My problem is that I don't have much of a self to explore. My life is too boring to serve as the focus of an extended exploration paper. I'm afraid if I make exploring *me* the subject of a paper I'll have very little to say."

How would you respond to Paula?

3. The informal exploratory essay often allows for multiple narrative frames to be placed around the telling of an event and a description of one's feelings about that event. Consider, for example, this selection from an essay in which Dana describes taking care of her grandmother, who suffered from Alzheimer's disease, a degenerative neural disease in which memory and higher cognitive functions progressively deteriorate. The starting point for Dana's essay is a description of the times her grandmother often wandered off and got lost and an effort to explore and communicate the feelings these episodes created in Dana.

As long as she stayed in the neighborhood, it wasn't a problem. But I felt sort of stupid inching my Jeep down the street, as if I'd lost my dog, yelling "Granny!" Every Wednesday morning I'd take her to another bluehair who specialized in bluehair and always arrive back promptly at 10 a.m. with a crisp ten dollar bill for the bluehair and a Slowpoke for Granny. But one time Motts was out of Slowpokes and I had to hunt one down at Winn-Dixie and didn't get to Granny until 10:05. It was too late. Poof! One gone Granny. Now, there were things Granny did that were irritating--like coming in my bedroom at 4 a.m. and asking me what's for lunch, and gee, it sure is dark outside isn't it? Must be a storm coming---and there were things Granny did that were depressing--like putting on her nightgown and waiting in bed for her boyfriend all day--but nothing compared to the sheer terror Granny could fill you with when she wandered off or you came home and found all four burners on high on the stove with a pan of grease in her hand. "What are you cooking, Granny?" An especially interesting question since there was never anything in the pan except grease, which no matter where I hid it, she could always find.

But this particular Wednesday I would have gladly traded one Granny playing with the stove in the house for one Granny on the loose. Since I had come another way, I decided to try the way home first and I'll be damned if there wasn't this beautifully coiffed old woman, striding purposely down the street, for all the years of carrying books up and down stairs and driving a Mack truck bookmobile, coming home only to milk a cow, canning all summer, going back out for PTA meetings and library meetings during the school year, hadn't made a dent in her body. It was only her mind that was totaled. I pulled up beside her and yelled for her to get in, but she didn't recognize me until I stopped the car and jumped out waving the Slowpoke. In that instant, when I hugged her tightly to my chest, I finally knew what my Mother had meant when I came home from playing far too late one night to find her face smashed into her pillow, sobbing. "Why are you crying, Mom?" "You'll understand when you have a child someday." Standing there, holding Granny, tears bouncing off the waxy Slowpoke wrapper, I realized I had a child all right. A child becoming more childlike everyday.

What is your sense of this essay as an exploratory essay? What freedoms of style and nuance does the exploratory essay allow Dana that a descriptive or expository essay might not? What is your impression of this essay? How does it affect you? What parts do you feel are the most effective for communicating Dana's feelings? What metaphors, images, analogies enable this essay to work for you? Does Dana use components of memory and visual imagery to convey her feelings about this experience and about her grandmother? Where and how, and are these instances effective?

If someone were to say to you, after reading Dana's essay, "Feelings, sentiments, and memories are fine in a letter, a diary, or a journal entry, but not in an essay," how would you respond?

4. Considering Dana's essay once more, how would you compare it with Eiseley's essay? Are they similar in style or tone? What about the impact they seek to make upon the reader--do you find similarities there? Based upon Eiseley's and Dana's essays, are there general conclusions you can come to about the nature of the informal exploratory essay? Further, if someone were to say to you that there can be no general pattern or contour to an exploratory essay because each deals with an examination of self and each person's self and set of experiences and memories are unique, how would you respond?

5. Vincent has finished his workbook exercises and says to you, "I think this idea of thinking of your life like it was a movie is ridiculous. What does that mean, anyway?"

How would you respond?

What ideas from *CHAPTER TEN: EXPLORING* (in either your textbook or your workbook) helped you the most with your writing? What ideas or techniques did you hope to get from this chapter but did not? What steps do you intend to take to learn those ideas or techniques?

"RESEARCH IS THE TRUEST TEST OF THE PRAGMATIC MIND"

--COLLIER GRYFELT

CHAPTER ELEVEN: WRITING A RESEARCH PAPER

Free Writing #1

What does the concept of writing a research paper mean to you? What ideas (or memories) come to mind?

Free Writing #2

Do you feel there is value to writing a research paper? What might that value be?

A research paper helps us address the question of *why*. It responds to and addresses our curiosity about a given subject, helping us extend our range of knowledge beyond what we already know into the area of what we can find out and discover. A research paper provides us the opportunity to extend our historical range, to move into the historical past and draw from previous eras insights and data that will help us explain our present concerns.

Interestingly, though, most people's view of a research paper is very negative. They perceive the activity of writing a research paper as one of the more drab and unexciting experiences they can imagine. Perhaps they were overzealously hounded by instructors who told them the essence of good research was the 3 x 5 note card. Perhaps they recall volumes and volumes of journal articles and books they had to read and felt they never could assimilate. Perhaps the idea of confronting volumes of printed research on a given topic made them feel they were inadequate intellectually and had little of value to contribute.

Whatever the cause, most people definitely do not associate a sense of joy, curiosity, and discovery with the research paper, and that is truly a disappointing phenomenon since joining the past and the present in new insights can be an invigorating challenge and an exciting prospect. As your textbook points out, the process is often recursive in that one item of information leads to a search for another, and assumptions that you thought were valid might be called into question as new data arise. In addition, a research paper addresses three concerns associated with critical thinking: the ability to identify and define a problem, to propose solutions to a problem, and to communicate one's findings to a general or a specialized audience. The research paper allows opportunities to improve skills in all three of these areas.

The essence of writing a research paper allows you to draw upon skills you have learned in previous sections of your course, your textbook, and your workbook. The skills you learned in keeping a journal will prove handy in keeping your research log, and your capacities to observe, remember, infer, explain, argue, and describe will be invaluable. Perhaps the most significant skill of all will be that of exploring, for research requires a dedicated commitment to exploring the fullest implications of your topic. This is again why it is important in the research paper, as in all essays, to narrow your topic so that you have a manageable area within which to focus your ideas and allow your talents to work to their fullest.

Free Writing #3

What type of audience or audiences do you think a research paper is aimed at? Why do you think so? What values underlie your assumptions? What line of reasoning leads you to your conclusions?

Group Exercise #1

Let the class engage in researching the topic of why a trend has occurred. Any trend in any historical era is fair game for this exercise, which focuses upon an exploration for the reasons behind the popularity of given fads or trends.

After the class has completed this exercise and discussed its results, let the class work on developing a set of guidelines on what constitutes trends, how they influence and are influenced by society, and what causes the decline and eventual disappearance of a trend? Let the class formulate, too, a general sense of how a topic of this type--which draws upon identification, definition, a sense of historical periods and changes, speculation, and drawing reasonable inferences from the data of historical eras--can or should be researched.

Exercise #1

Consider Group Exercise #1 and evaluate how you would go about presenting your information on trends to an audience. What methods would you use for appealing to your readers' interests and concerns? What type of balance would you want to maintain between research from historical sources and original insights and perceptions not influenced by external research? How would you go about attaining this balance?

Free Writing #4

What insights into your own composing processes would writing a research paper give you? What would you learn about yourself as a writer?

One of the great advantages of a research paper in many people's minds is that it allows a person to go beyond his or her own knowledge and experience and integrate the views and ideas of others. Obviously, integrating the views of many other authors and citing a series of sources to substantiate one's points create difficulties in terms of form and organization. Working in massive amounts of material into your research paper can overwhelm an audience, particularly if your paper becomes a listing (points 1 2 3 4, etc.) of major ideas. Leaving out crucial ideas, though, can be equally as detrimental since your audience is likely to doubt the value of your work and to question how thoroughly you have researched your subject with dedication and sincerity.

Many students as beginning writers are tempted to follow the most formulaic of structures for their papers. Essentially, they produce a paper that looks like they have taken 3 x 5 note cards, stapled them together, and typed up the results. Not only is such a paper simplistic in design, it reads poorly since no audience can be bombarded for long with quotation after quotation without hungering for some insight and some break in the tedium of one sustained approach. More sophisticated writers still rely quite heavily upon the research they have done prior to writing their papers, but, in the actual writing, they depend upon interesting and varied ways to incorporate their research data into their writing. A high premium is placed upon transitions amongst ideas and upon a style that varies in response to reader need.

If you were designing guidelines to instruct others on how to write a research paper, you would probably come up with a sequence not too different from the traditional method. Certainly you would encourage people to choose topics that interested them, since enthusiasm will carry a long way during an extensive research project. Even within assigned topics, such an option is possible. If a student is assigned a research paper on "Excessive Governmental Intervention into the Private Sector" and she is a pre-med major, she might want to direct the focus of her paper toward considering ways in which governmental constraints affect doctors in private practice. Thus, even though the topic is an assigned one, she can choose a slant or a direction that allows her to be enthusiastic about the paper she will be writing.

Second, you would encourage writers of research papers to narrow their topics into a manageable form. To write upon "Gender" would be impossible in the scope of the traditional 15-20 page research paper. Writing upon "Gender Discrimination in Housing Patterns in America during 1975-85" would be much more manageable.

Third, you would encourage your people to begin their research by initially reading on a broad subject and then narrowing their topic. The reading on a broad subject should be used to encourage curiosity and to stimulate creative thinking about the topic--a seed bed from which other inspirations will grow.

Fourth, you would suggest that your researchers begin the actual process of tracking down information, including learning to use the card catalogue and a range of other informational sources related to the disciplines they are studying. If they are researching a topic in science, they will use different indexes and information retrieval sources than if they are researching a topic in literature or the fine arts.

Becoming aware of the resources available to them in their library would also be an important aspect of this phase, enhancing their knowledge of the field and its body of research data.

You would advise your people that, when they wrote their papers, they should engage the reader's interest quickly and sustain that interest through careful organization and well-structured sentences. The research from other sources should be worked into the paper in such a fashion as to indicate craft with the use of external sources, rather than making external sources themselves the entire paper. And certainly you would advise careful proofreading and editing, including a check of one's sources that were quoted. After you completed giving out our guidelines, you would feel confident in asserting that any individual who followed this set of guidelines would have a better chance of producing a well-structured and well-developed research paper than one who undertook the project in a hit or miss fashion.

Group Exercise #2

Divide the class into groups based upon academic majors or interests, and have each group describe the ideal process for conducting research in its discipline. Each group should note valuable reference sources, as well as discuss the issues involved in researching data in its field.

In phase two of the assignment, let each group outline a plan of research for its discipline and exchange that plan with another group. The second group will then follow the guidelines laid down by the first group and comment upon its accuracy and value to a lay person outside that field or discipline. If difficulties arise in following out the research plan, the second group will advise on changes to be made to clarify the procedure and make it more accessible to others.

Among the research skills important to all disciplines are the ability to summarize and paraphrase information. Long quotations especially invite being summarized or paraphrased, since the material contained in the quotation is difficult for a reader to take in easily; therefore, it advantages the writer to clarify for the reader and to highlight the key points involved rather than to duplicate the quotation in its entirety. Beginning writers often neglect this aspect of writing the research paper, and, as a result, their papers become a compendium of long quotations. The effect upon the reader is often a numbing one, since volumes of material are thrown at the reader without a clue as to how the material should be weighted or interpreted.

In this regard, a good concept to borrow here from journalism is the idea of the headline. Headlines allow the reader to weigh what news is most important, simply by the size of the headline. The assumption is that the larger the type on the headline of a story, the more significant that story is. If all headlines were of the same size type, it would be harder for the reader to distinguish this hierarchy of importance amongst all the stories presented in the newspaper. In a similar fashion, if all of the quotations in a research paper are long, then the reader can assume that all are of equal value or merit to the paper's argument. If, on the other hand, one uses quotations with skill and design, one indicates to the reader that this passage quoted at length is important to interpret and understand in its entirety, while another passage, though important, can be paraphrased so that the reader can get the essence of the idea. Careful use of paraphrase and summary, together with long quotations, makes the reader more aware of how to evaluate the information presented.

A central concern in writing research papers is the issue of plagiarism, which is defined as knowingly using another person's words or ideas without giving proper credit to that person. Most students are not guilty of direct or overt plagiarism in that they purposefully set out to steal another person's ideas and claim them as their own; these instances are truly the rare examples. Instead, they are guilty of indirect plagiarism in that they quote material and do not know how (or neglect) to give proper credit for the material through footnotes and citations in the bibliography. This type of indirect plagiarism created through carelessness or ignorance is quite common, but it still gives the reader the impression that someone else's ideas are your own. Whether the plagiarism has been direct or indirect, the penalties are often very severe, so students are urged to be careful in properly citing their sources and giving full credit to material they are quoting from an external source.

Exercise #2

Discuss the issue of plagiarism. Why do you feel it is an important issue in terms of research and in writing the research paper? What guidelines would you encourage others to follow in understanding the significance of carefully documented research in order to avoid issues of plagiarism?

Students often question the value of research papers, insisting instead that they prefer to write from their own ideas rather than simply paraphrase or cite other writers. While this concept has a great deal of romantic appeal to it, the fact is that college writing assignments often require that students respond to material they have read with critical interpretations and evaluations. Students will be called upon to analyze, synthesize, draw inferences from, and substantiate conclusions about the material they have read. Often these last two steps in the procedure are enhanced by one's ability to cite sources and to bring additional research concepts into play.

It is interesting to note that often good research skills begin with good critical reading and thinking skills. Obviously, if you do not know how to read a passage and get the main ideas from it, you will have little success in interpreting that passage and its key concepts for your readers. Your ability to communicate depends upon a triad of skills involving reading, interpreting, and communicating. All work together to enable you to convey information to a reader interested in learning more about the topic you have researched.

Interestingly, all the skills you have brought to bear in other writing assignments also apply to the research paper; even though many people feel that the research paper is somehow separate from all other kinds of writing, the truth is that for the research paper, as in all writing tasks, one needs to understand the assignment, consider the audience, generate ideas through free writings, brainstorming, or any of the other methods discussed in previous chapters, develop a thesis and a line of approach to that thesis that personalizes the topic for the writer, organize a sense of the paper's structure, draft, revise, edit, and proofread. To this fundamental structure are added the additional components of: (1) length--most research papers are generally three to four times the length of other non-research assignments; (2) time--most research papers are written over a much more extended period of time (sometimes over an entire semester) than the average writing assignment that might have a deadline of one class period to one week before it is due; (3) sources--research papers require the incorporation of outside references to back up the ideas presented and to show the depth of consideration and the range of opinions that have been given to a particular topic; and (4) documentation--research papers require footnotes or internal citations, as well as a full list of works cited at the end of the paper, to indicate the sources from which the writer has drawn the supporting ideas for his or her research paper. While these four considerations *seem* to make the research paper somehow unique amongst writing assignments, it is important to note that these four concepts are added onto a very familiar writing pattern of coming up with an idea, organizing it for a given audience, and writing the final version of the work with style, clarity, and grace of expression. Think of the research paper as a basic writing assignment to which new facets have been added--much like one adds new rooms to an enduring, tried and true house--and the idea of writing a research paper will seem far less intimidating and far more manageable.

Since research papers do require more time to write, it is wise to plan out one's approach and to break the task down into manageable, sequential units. Allowing ample time to complete each unit of the process takes away a lot of anxiety associated with finishing the research paper; in addition, the completion of each section builds your confidence and encourages you to complete the next step. It is important to remember, too, in this process that the all of the stages have the potential to be recursive. That is, while completing stage three, you might find additional ideas or insights that you might then wish to go back and incorporate into stages one and two. This is a natural aspect of research papers, as it is of all writing assignments, and it is one that is to be welcomed for the creativity and depth it brings to your writing. Thus, don't be disturbed, but heartened, if you discover that each stage sheds a degree of new light upon previous stages. You might find that your greatest creativity and insights reside in this very factor.

The ability to narrow a topic is crucial to writing a research paper, and, even though the recursive nature of writing and the joy involved in researching a topic to its fullest often encourage students to expand their topics, it is a far wiser course of action to follow if you narrow your topic and then work within that framework to research as fully as you can. Otherwise, the topic will get away from you and out of control because, realistically, no one can fully research a broad and abstract topic to fit into the scope and intent of a research paper. Libraries are full of books and articles on such broad topics, and, since even one book does not fully cover all the aspects of a broad topic, how can you expect to do so in ten to twenty pages? So, rule #1: narrow your topic *before* you do your research. If you begin your research and find that you wish to alter your original topic slightly based upon new information you have discovered, still be very careful to stay within manageable parameters. If you decide to write on "The Elderly," that is too broad; if you decide on "Nursing Home Care for the Elderly," that is much narrower; and if, in the course of researching your topic, you decide upon "Nursing Home Care for the Elderly on Medicaid," you have changed your original topic slightly, but you have also narrowed it, too, rather than expanding it into a topic that cannot be handled adequately within the scope of a research paper.

Exercise #3

Consider the general topics below and narrow them down into topics suitable for a research paper.

* The Vietnam War

* Science fiction

* Political elections

* Gardening

* Skin Cancer

* New Cars

* Computer Technology

* Psychoanalysis

* Sexually Transmitted Diseases

* Aging

216

Once you have specified the topic for your research paper, you are ready to begin gathering information about it. You have a number of potential sources of information, depending upon your topic. Certainly, one of the most potent in terms of impact upon a reader is the *interview*. In an interview, you are presenting an individual's viewpoint, and often the colloquial manner in which an individual might phrase his or her perceptions can be more exciting and interesting than purely depending upon library sources. Interviews, after all, give a measure of immediacy and intimacy to your presentation of the facts surrounding an issue.

Do not fall into the mistaken notion that your interviews have to be with experts in the field, when, actually, there is a great deal of power in the oral history of everyday individuals. If, for example, you decided to write upon aging as your topic, interviews with nurses and doctors in nursing homes would be very effective, but do not underestimate the power of talking with the elderly persons who reside in the nursing homes and can give very moving accounts of what it means to grow old in America, a society that places a high premium upon youth and innocence versus age and experience. If you are writing a paper on economic recessions, don't overlook talking with your relatives and their friends who have lived through periods of economic downturns. Their stories might lend an air of authenticity and interest to your research paper that no other source could.

Exercise #4

Select a topic and then write out a set of questions that you could use in an interview designed to elicit information about that topic. Be sure to specify the type of person you would be interviewing, your reasons for selecting that person, and the goals or aims of the questions you are asking in terms of (relationship to) your topic.

By far, the most often used source of reference material for research papers is the library. To use the library effectively, which will serve as the source of some of your most important explorations during your academic career, it is important to know where everything is located in your library. If you have not visited your college library or your public library, do so. Be sure to acquaint yourself with your library's method for organizing information. Some libraries use the Dewey Decimal system, some the Library of Congress classification method, while some libraries use a combination of the two. Some libraries have card catalogues, while other libraries have computerized systems for locating books and for information retrieval. The holdings and facilities of libraries differ from place to place, and it is important for you to learn your library well in order to use its contents well and as an aid to your research. Knowing your library well is also a great time saver, keeping you from spending hours in the stacks looking for a volume of a journal that your library doesn't even subscribe to, and other assorted horrors associated with fruitless library searches that could have become fruitful had the person known what he or she was doing in using the library's resources.

Group Exercise #3

Let the class divide into groups. Each group will be responsible for visiting the library and writing a user's guide to a particular aspect of the library's offerings or holdings. One group might describe how one goes about using government documents, while another might describe the use of the interlibrary loan facilities.

Let the groups present their user's guide and have it critiqued for clarity by the class as a whole. When that aspect has been completed, let each group distribute its guide to members of the other groups and see how easily others can use the guide to locate the information or to use the facilities described in the guide.

Conducting your library research is very much like being a detective searching for clues. Each reference source in the library has the potential to lead you to new sources, and each will, in turn, suggest potential new approaches you can take to your topic to flesh out your initial ideas. The most general sources of information about a topic are usually encyclopedias and general dictionaries, like biographical dictionaries or dictionaries of philosophy. Because the information in these works is so general and, therefore, often rather sketchy, most instructors do not consider encyclopedias and general reference dictionaries as the best of research sources. Many teachers will specify that you may quote from an encyclopedia or general reference dictionary only once in your research paper, or set up some other standard for use. While these reference sources may not be considered the best or the fullest by some people, they do represent a good starting place for many people just beginning their research.

From this initial introduction to your topic, the search strategy becomes the best method for exploration of your topic in greater depth. After the encyclopedias in the reference section, use the *Library of Congress Subject Headings* to find card catalogue subject headings; locate indexes to periodicals, newspapers, book reviews, bibliographies, and doctoral dissertations; and check government documents. Never forget the value, too, of the serendipitous finding of information, since a great deal of what you find out can often be by lucky coincidence or chance. After you locate the book on your subject, browse in the stacks for a few moments and look at the related books on your topic or on topics similar to yours. Remember that many books and articles contain reference sources of their own contained in bibliographies at the end of the work, and each of these bibliographies can also point you in new directions as you search for source materials to document and support your views. Some libraries have facilities for computer-based reference searches, which are excellent sources of research information because of their speed, efficiency, and thoroughness.

How you go about organizing the information you locate is a matter of personal preference, unless you are given specific instructions by your teacher to turn in your reference sources in a particular manner. Some people make note cards, on which they list all the bibliographic information for the particular reference, plus a brief summary of the main ideas or a key quotation they intend to use in their paper. Others keep a journal of reading notes complete with bibliographic citations. In this journal, they jot down key ideas and/or thoughts and concepts that come to them as they read the original source. Others photocopy each research item and then make notes in the margin as they read. Whichever of these ways works best for you and you find more comfortable is the most important issue, since any or all provide very effective ways for keeping track of the information you discover.

Once the information has been gathered for your paper, it is time to write your first draft. Rarely are students successful when they try to skip the drafting stage and create a perfect paper the first time through. Your first draft enables you to reconsider your argument: have you narrowed your topic sufficiently? have you explored your topic in sufficient depth? does your paper read logically, or are there gaps in the development and interconnection of your ideas? It also provides you with an opportunity to consider your style and its clarity of expression, as well as your sense of the right style, tone, and voice to adopt for your audience.

A valid question, though, is how does one conceptualize a research paper, since this stage would obviously come before the writing of a draft. Students generally find two approaches helpful. One is the more traditional approach of integrating one's sources into the draft as one writes and formulates a sense of the structure of the paper [the approach discussed in your textbook], and the other is the less conventional, but still utilitarian, approach of writing the draft first, as if it were a typical essay, and then incorporating the research into the draft at key points that necessitate and involve substantiation through reference sources.

One way to understand this second approach is to think of it as a form of annotating a text. Annotating, which generally involves underlining sentences and passages or making notes in the margins of a text, serves two purposes: (1) to record a reader's reactions to a text and (2) to organize the text in such a way that future study and review are made easier. In either instance, annotating highlights key ideas, examples, and quotations, pointing out the most essential elements of that given text.

In terms of the research paper, a variant of annotating can be used as a very important invention and organizational tool. After the writer has written his or her version of the paper as if it were an essay, he or she goes back and marks (annotates) those sections of the draft/essay that could better be elaborated upon, expanded, clarified, and substantiated through the addition of references to external sources. Partly this process will involve one's ability to recognize major ideas within a text and how these ideas can be given more depth and weight through citations to other sources, and partly this process involves what your textbook describes as "using sources to make *Your* point."

Many students are tempted, for a variety of reasons, to let sources take over their paper. When they write from the traditional method, they wind up with a series of quotations and very little true text of their own. With the second approach, the student first generates a text of his or her own and then uses sources to expand upon, support, and clarify key ideas within the text.

A student, for example, is writing about literacy education in America. She may begin in the traditional fashion by citing sources and statistical data to substantiate the viewpoint that verbal skills have been declining in America for the last two decades. She may further bolster this claim by quoting passages and summarizing or paraphrasing other sources relevant to the key issues associated with the assessment of educational objectives and outcomes. At this point, she may wish to work in a degree of personal narrative that centers upon her experiences in the American educational system. That is, if she can. Many students find themselves overwhelmed at this point and feeling as if they should continue citing sources. They find it difficult to find ways to integrate their personal opinions into the text, or even to believe that their opinions or narratives of their personal experiences have much value.

Using the alternative approach, this same student could write a draft of her research paper by making her experiences in the educational system the core of her paper, annotating key ideas, and then, in response to her annotations, supporting her ideas with references. Her paper might begin, for example, with the statement, "As a student, I found elementary school thrilling; by junior high, a certain malaise had set in; and, by high school, I was both profoundly bored and distressed with the education I was receiving."

At this point, the student circles *bored* and writes in the margin, Neeley, p. 60; 75%, which is a shorthand note to herself to include after this sentence a reference to an article by Robert Finn Neeley on why students drop out of school, in which Neeley states on page 60 of the article that 75% of high school students polled indicated that they were bored with the education they were receiving.

The student may put in her annotations as she writes the draft, or she may complete the entire draft and then go back and put in her annotations. If the reference sources are known, as in the example with Neeley, she can cite them in the annotation. If not, she can make a note to herself, something like "Look for source on how other high school students feel about the education they are receiving."

The exercises that follow will provide you with opportunities to apply these techniques to sample essays. Each essay that follows represents a draft that starts off as a personal essay to which annotations on reference sources can be added. Applying this technique to these essays will teach you a valuable tool (and skill) for structuring research papers. It will show you, too, that there is no one correct way to write a draft of a research paper, there are only ways that are effective and that work. For each writer of a research paper, what works to "get the creative juices flowing" and to make the draft come together will be different, and part of becoming a good writer, whether of research papers or of any type of composition, is finding out what works for you and then applying that knowledge with skill, patience, and craft. The

Greek philosophers wrote above the doorway to the temple of wisdom, "Know thyself," and this truth applies to writing as well. Whether it is writing rituals or trying the technique of annotating to write a draft of a research paper, knowing what techniques work for you to get you writing and keep you writing well is 80% of the battle.

Exercise #5

The following essay represents an initial phrasing, in draft form, of what will be a research paper on applying the views of German philosopher Martin Heidegger to an analysis of N. Scott Momaday's *The Way to Rainy Mountain*. Your assignment is to annotate the text in such a fashion that you are indicating in the margins the *types* of references the student might wish to cite to broaden, substantiate, or clarify her views. [Note that *types* here does not mean an encyclopedia, a newspaper article, etc., but whether the student should search for a reference on theories of self, additional discussions of Heidegger's philosophy, discussions of the major themes in Momaday's book, etc. In this manner, make the annotations as specific as possible with regard to what information the student should research, and this will help give you a fuller sense of how the technique of annotation works for a research paper and whether you might find it a valuable approach for your own writing assignments that require research.]

Philosophies of Being

Even in the darkness, there are differences. The moonlight illuminates the flat, planted row, while the still untamed earth appears as a sea of black. My being transposes itself into sight, perceiving differences for the sake of description. The scene exists only because I exist. Another being may not notice the moonlight or the subtle differences in the earth's surface. Another being may not go to her garden to ponder what it is to be.

Heidegger believes one exists "to be"; to ask, "What is it, to be?" What is interesting, however, is that he provides an answer, a way/method/model of being even as he claims being can only be what one is. Once he describes being, have we not, then, been distracted by his definition, so as to be predisposed to believe pondering "being" is the only way we can truly be? *Being and Time* is Heidegger's attempt to transcend finiteness, but he makes both terms finite by definition. Being is time, time is being. We only exist because of time. Time only exists because we exist. But having said that, why say anything more? Why tell us that "to be" is to ask, "What is it, to be?" and then spend 488 pages explaining what being IS? Surely he must have known that by explaining, by using language, by recording his thoughts

221

in writing on paper, he was creating an absolute, even as the invisible enemy of his diatribe is absolutism. But then, perhaps, it is my being that gives Heidegger's being absoluteness. Heidegger would say that I am "free" to perceive his being only through my own being, that he isn't absolute anymore than my being perceives him to be, that even to differentiate between his being and my being is to perceive differentiation exists.

Perhaps such was also the intent of N. Scott Momaday in *The Way To Rainy Mountain*. Even before one begins to read, one notices three separate paragraphs on the page, distinctly set apart, as if one would not note the differences in "voice" without the white space, like the molded ridges that compartmentalize TV dinners, keeping the "myth" from "reality," our peas from our potatoes. Thus, the eye predisposes us to separation before the ear has even begun to hear. Of course, as Heidegger points out in "The Origin of the Work of Art" in *Poetry, Language, Thought*, my sight renders the words on the page as "nothing but the unity of a manifold of what is given the senses." Such is also true for the way in which my ear differentiates the voices. The first voice is mythic, seemingly imaginary. The second is historical, apparently factual. The third is personal, a glimpse of the intimate. But, once again, my being has given whatever form Momaday meant to present my own distinct definition. I can only read Momaday's being through my own being. It is my perception of what the words mean, my perception of how Momaday is using language, that "names" the voices as distinct. "Language, by naming beings for the first time, first brings beings to word and to appearance. Only this naming nominates beings *to* their being from out of *their being*." But maybe what one's senses perceive is precisely what Momaday meant for the reader to experience. Maybe one perceives separation because that has been the existence of the Native American, who has been separated from his or her reality by the white man labeling that experience as "myth" while what's "true" is the white man's "factual" account. Or maybe Momaday, like Heidegger, isn't concerned with whether something is "true" or not by way of being mythic or factual. What's true is what's most personal. Thus, Momaday could be interpreted as saying that even as Native Americans view the white man's history with skepticism and bitterness, so must they realize that they, too, have certain conventions and literary traditions through which they explain their existence. A Kiowa who doesn't want to believe that the tribe originated from a hollow log is just as ostracized by his or her own people as Native Americans are ostracized by Anglo-Saxons.

Ultimately, as Heidegger says in *Being and Time*, "The question of existence never gets straightened out except through existing itself"; and so it is with *The Way To Rainy Mountain*, just as it is with my communion with my garden, or, rather, the plot of land I can see as already green and lush, spotted with specks of yellow and red, where others only see dirt. It's not living in a teepee or dancing around a campfire that makes one an Indian, just as it's not the need for food that makes one plant a garden. It's being one with the experience in such a way that the experience itself allows one to BE.

Now try this same assignment with sample essay #2.

The Self and the Journal

As in dreams, the unconscious self often speaks to itself before the conscious self happens to overhear. Yet, it is within this inner dialogue that much of what eventually makes its way to canvas, film or a musical score gestates before giving birth to itself. Yet, much is also lost, for even to linguistically assume an unconscious separate from a conscious mind is to separate the self from itself, the creator from the created.

While writing itself is a linguistic construct, a journal still offers the creator an opportunity to not only communicate what she proposes to create, but what the Self is creating in the creator. Certainly, journals do not and should not be limited to writing, but instead should express whatever "language" the Self feels most comfortable using. Whatever the form, it is the content that is most important. For within the contents of the creator as mirrored in the journal, lie the contents of what has yet to be created.

Group Exercise #4

This exercise follows the same pattern as Exercise #5. The class, in groups or as a whole, is to annotate the following text by indicating the types of references the student might wish to cite. Let the class be as specific as possible in suggesting and detailing the types of references that would benefit the paper the most.

Loneliness in John Steinbeck's "The Chrysanthemums"

John Steinbeck's "The Chrysanthemums" explores the question of loneliness and of how each individual will deal with the emotional emptiness he or she experiences in life. The concept of loneliness is embodied in the character of Elisa Allen, a young woman who is represented by Steinbeck as out of place with her social circumstances. Elisa is married to a man who treats her with respect and gentleness, but who fails to understand her deepest, burning passion to be more free in life. As a further symbol of her isolation, Elisa puts her faith in an itinerant tinker by revealing her secret feelings and wishes to him, only to have the tinker literally throw away the gift of chrysanthemums she has given him, as a symbol of his disregard.

Steinbeck opens the story with a scene that is a metaphor for Elisa's state in life. Elisa is alone in her garden, while her husband and several other men conduct the business of the farm. There is an interesting symbolic split here between men's work (and a man's world) and woman's work (and a woman's world). On the surface, the scene represents simple domesticity and conventional sex role behaviors, with the man handling the business of the farm and its financial matters, while the woman "putters" in her garden. However, the reader soon discovers that Elisa is not the typical image of domesticity and conventional sex role behavior that the reader might first believe. Elisa is described as a large woman with mannish features, and she is not out in her garden like a typical housewife contentedly planting flowers as a frivolous hobby. Instead, she is working in her garden as a means of spiritual survival. Into the garden she places the energy she might place into her marriage and into loving her husband, if she were able. Into the garden, too, she places the great restlessness of her spirit that seems to overwhelm her at times.

As Elisa works in her chrysanthemum garden, an itinerant tinker appears, looking for work. Symbolically, he is the first, and only, visitor in the story from the male world who is allowed into Elisa's garden. This factor is a key element in the themes that Steinbeck wishes to portray, for the fact that Elisa allows a man into her garden is indicative of the fact that she has let a man get close to her at all.

Because Elisa sees (or at least thinks she sees) in the tinker, and the lifestyle he possesses, a symbol of the life she herself would like to lead, she feels an instant empathy with the tinker. She, too, would like to live by impulse, traveling here and there whenever she pleased. She would like to be free of the farm and of her expected and confining role in life as a typical farm housewife, but all she can do is dream and long, for, as the tinker says to her, "It ain't the right kind of life for a woman." Elisa immediately responds, "How do you know? How can you tell?" The fiery bitterness of Elisa's remark indicates the intensity of the frustration Elisa feels. It also indicates that she feels that no man can fully understand her, for no man can truly understand her desire to be free of the confining role she feels she is trapped in as a typical female in the American 1930's.

The fact that the tinker would take an interest in Elisa's garden makes Elisa feel a closeness to the tinker that is emotional and also frightening. At a key moment in their talk together, Elisa wants to reach out and place her hand on the tinker's leg. Not only would this gesture be a violation of Elisa's marriage vows, for she is feeling sexual passion for another man, but it would be, too, a violation of the limitations of her sex role--for women in the 1930's were not supposed to make overtures to men. Such an action, in contrast to today, would represent a dramatic severing of Elisa's ties to her femininity. But she cannot fully break the ties, which is indicative of her frustration in the story. Like the chrysanthemums, Elisa is a rare flower--a beautiful combination of strong growth and natural beauty and passion. But, just like the chrysanthemums, she is also rooted in place. Ironically, she is dependent upon men for the only release from her frustrating life that she finds. It is the tinker who will carry away a piece of Elisa's spirit by taking a pot of chrysanthemums, and it is Elisa's husband who will take her to town in the car to offer her a chance at a diminished dream of romance--a fine meal in a restaurant with some wine.

Before Elisa leaves the farm with her husband, though, she enacts a cleaning ritual that is symbolic of her emotional state. Feeling frightened, and perhaps cheapened or ashamed of her feelings for the tinker, Elisa tries to suppress the true nature of her emotions. She scrubs at herself harshly with soap until her skin almost bleeds, and she dresses up, perfumes herself, and makes up her face to assume the conventional image expected of women in this era. Her husband is amazed when he sees her, yet is unable to express his feelings, leaving Elisa feeling even more lonely and frustrated. Trying to please her husband with her femininity, Elisa finds, instead, that it drives an even deeper wedge of lack of communication between them.

Dissatisfied with her husband's response, Elisa nonetheless goes into town, hoping the night out will fulfill her. Instead, she finds her worst and saddest fear confirmed--the tinker has thrown away the chrysanthemums she gave him. He was not truly interested in her at all, only in the job and the money she provided him. Her chrysanthemums, symbolic of a piece of her soul, were only so much garbage to pitch away, while the pot they were in (which Elisa regarded as of little value) was important to the tinker as a material object because he could sell it or trade it for other items he wanted. While Elisa's values were spiritual and emotional (empathetic), the tinker's were purely materialistic. Thus, his actions show Elisa that he, too, is in a world different from her own and that she is even more isolated than she imagined. Further, Elisa is forced by the tinker's actions to see her empty life more clearly and to experience her loneliness on a much deeper and much more poignant level. Thus, the movement of the story can be seen as a symbolic progression of one day in Elisa Allen's life that also represents the sadness of her spirit and the dissatisfaction she feels with her life.

Through images and details of isolation and lack of communication in "The Chrysanthemums," John Steinbeck captures the poignancy of Elisa's efforts to come to terms with her emotionally unsatisfying life. Steinbeck could have created a much more conventional and simplistic story by providing easy answers to Elisa's dilemma; instead, he portrays a woman trapped in a world that is not fulfilling to her, and yet unable to find any real way out other than restless longing and the shelter of fantasies, daydreams, and wishes.

Group Exercise #5

The traditional approach to writing a research paper involves the incorporating of one's references into the text as one writes the draft. The paper that follows represents such an approach and is representative of how researched material works within the conceptual framework of a research paper.

Let the class, in groups or as a whole, critique the following paper for its content, style, organization, the quality of its research, and for how cohesively the researched material has been worked into the main ideas the paper wishes to present. [Note that this paper is using the 1985 MLA style of internal citations to indicate its reference sources, all of which are detailed in the *Works Cited* section that follows at the end of the paper.]

Literature as Political Theory

The theme, "the personal is political," has been, and continues to be, inextricably woven into the women's movement, as well as women's literature. But, as Betty Friedan's phrase, "the second stage" suggests, this idea is hardly new. Just as the 1972 introduction of the Equal Rights Amendment was not the first time such legislation for equality between the sexes was proposed, so the "personal is political" concept is not strictly a post-1960's metaphor. Charlotte Perkins Gilman proposed the idea in 1898 in her treatise for women's economic liberation and independence, *Women and Economics*. In so doing, Gilman "anticipated the direction of some of the most recent and perceptive feminist theorists: the concentration on the politics of the family, for example, the recognition that the personal is political, the understanding that only by examining the daily lives of women and their experiences of submission to the demands of family life could an explanation of female 'difference' ultimately be found" (Hill 516).

For Gilman, explaining the female "difference" substantiated her belief that differentiation ultimately leads to segregation, division of labor, and sex-role stereotyping. As a result, Gilman believed, "the machinery of society does not function as cooperatively and efficiently as it should because half the human race is not allowed to participate freely in the productivity of society" (Magner 71). Influenced by Lester Ward and Edward Bellamy, Gilman's beliefs were not so much feminist as humanist in that she was concerned with the collective good of humanity; thus, "keeping half the adult population at primitive, undifferentiated tasks retarded human progress and evolution as a whole" (Magner 72).

Perhaps this distinction explains why Gilman felt the need to include men in what would otherwise be a glorious celebration of female, self-sufficient exclusivity: Herland, a society so foreign to the patriarchaly educated mind that Elizabeth Keyser can only describe it as "at best limited, incomplete, and at worst, inhuman" (40).

It seems rather incongruous that Keyser should characterize Herland as inhuman when Van, the male narrator of the novel, describes it as "a civilization in which untroubled peace, the unmeasured plenty, the steady health, the large good will and smooth management which ordered everything, left nothing to overcome" (Gilman 99). Certainly Keyser would not want to imply that Herland was inhuman simply because of its small number of male characters, for Gilman's female characters are far too accepting and, to some extent, even accommodating, of their three male visitors--Terry, the archetypal patriarchal male; Jeff, the romantic; and Van, the sensitive mediator--to be considered inhuman. Further, the Herlanders marry their three male visitors, a direct statement that Gilman's objections are not to men, per se, but to male-dominated societies.

Thus, perhaps Keyser's quarrel with Herland is not so much its lack of men as its lack of passion. Quoting Terry's remark that Herlanders have "neither the vices of men, nor the virtues of women--they're neuters!" and then Jeff's response that "these women have the virtue of humanity, with less of its faults," Keyser claims that "Jeff's defense of the Herlanders is more troubling to the reader than Terry's attack on them, for it leads one to ask whether they can really possess 'the virtues of humanity' while lacking passion. It is one thing to have a mind unclouded by passion; it is another to be incapable of feeling it" (40-41).

Keyser seems not only to assume that passion and reason are separate, but that reason is never passionate, and passion is never reasonable. Considering her patriarchal perspective, this distinction can be, and often is, true, but such is not the case in Herland. Distinctions, especially dichotomies, were precisely what Gilman sought to avoid in creating a society in which "the drama, the dance, music, religion, and education were all very close together; and instead of developing them in detached lines, they had kept the connection" (Gilman 99-100).

Unlike Western thought, which believes the only way one can study and, thus, understand life, is to continually break it down into parts, Gilman asserts life is best understood as a whole, a unity. Without dichotomies, Van observes, the Herlanders "had no theory of the essential opposition of good and evil; life to them was growth" (102). As such, everything in Herland is connected by the thread that interweaves the fabric of the entire society. Gilman's belief was that in "society, as for the multicellular body, the collective good represented not just 'altruism' but basic economic necessity," a perspective quite apart from the "rugged individualist" (Magner 71) view Americans traditionally have had of their society.

Ann Lane concurs with this view, claiming Gilman thought society's ideas about individualism "distort the most intimate human relationships; she offers instead a world in which a genuine sense of community triumphs and is expressed in richer, more gratifying relationships" (xiv). Individualism was not so much the true cause of Gilman's concern, however, so much as the inequality it caused between the sexes. Men were allowed to be individuals, women were not. As a result, Gilman, according to Lane, was often adamant in saying that "the most important fact about the sexes, men and women, is the common humanity we share, not the differences that distinguish us" (xi).

Ironically, though, despite her avowed intellectual positions, Gilman found it hard to completely escape gender differences. The vast majority of what little has been written about Gilman and her writing tends to focus on the paradoxes within her fiction, as well as her life. An unabashedly aggressive proponent of the natural superiority of women, Gilman, nevertheless, was constantly plagued by her conflict with a sense "that certain stereotypes of 'femininity' must somehow be innate" (Hill 518). Yet, in her short story, "The Yellow Wallpaper," Gilman rebels against this so-called femininity by placing her female protagonist in a nursery with bars on the windows and a bed that is nailed down to represent metaphorically the eternal child-like existence women are locked into, not by biology but by a man-made society that forbids women the opportunity to broaden their intellectual or sexual insight. In the final scene of the story, the narrator escapes what Gilman has likened to "female enslavement" (Hill 515) by going insane, crawling over her fainted husband in the same way men have walked over women since time immemorial. As Paula Treichler has pointed out, though, "The final vision itself is one of physical enslavement not liberation: the woman, bound by a rope, circles the room like an animal in a yoke" (74). The husband will eventually recover, returning to his superior role. The woman will not. For Gilman, community, rather than one sex or the other, should ultimately reign supreme. The focus of society should not concentrate on differences, but on similarities, on integration rather than separation. "To prove that a woman can love and work, too," Gilman wrote in a letter to her husband, "to resist this dragging weight of the old swollen woman-heart, and force it into place--the world's life first--my own life next. Work first--love next" (Hill 504). In *Herland*, Gilman creates a society in which everything is integrated--work, love, family, friendship, country--are all simultaneously meaningful to Herlanders. As Van observes, "They loved one another with a practically universal affection, rising to exquisite and unbroken friendships, and broadening to a devotion to their country and people for which our word patriotism is no definition at all" (Gilman 94). Contrary to what Keyser believes, working for the good of the country is a passion for the Herlanders. In fact, everything Herlanders do is undertaken with passionate zeal, so that matters of the head are not differentiated from matters of the heart, a trait that even good-natured Van finds hard to accept once married to Ellador, who cannot stop thinking of her community. "'We and 'we' and 'we'--it was so hard to get her to be personal. And, as I thought that, I suddenly remembered how we were always criticizing 'our' women for 'being' so personal," he first complains (126). He tries to tell her that he "hadn't married the nation. . . . But she only smiled at her own limitations and explained that she had to 'think in we's'" (129).

The supreme communal act of Herland is the raising of the children, for "children were the 'raison d'etre'" (51) of the country; and Herlanders were "Mothers, not in our sense of helpless involuntary fecundity, forced to fill and overfill the land, every land, and then see their children suffer, sin, and die, fighting horribly with one another; but in the sense of Conscious Makers of People. Mother-love with them was not a brute passion, a mere 'instinct,' a wholly personal feeling; it was--a religion" (68). Instead of having Nietzsche's "uberman" or "over-man," Herland has "over-mothers," or those who were allowed to bear more than one child in honor of their motherhood skills. Childbearing occurs through parthenogenesis, which makes for an interesting dilemma when, after marriage, the men are eager to consummate their love, while the Herlanders don't understand why lovemaking should be done for any purposes other than procreation.

"It develops love," Van explains. "All the power of beautiful permanent mated love comes through this higher development."

"Are you sure?" Ellador asks. "How do you know that it was so developed? There are some kinds of birds who love each other so that they mope and pine if separated, and never pair again if one dies, but they never mate except in the mating season. Among your people do you find high and lasting affection appearing in proportion to this indulgence?" (126).

In making such comparisons, one could argue that Gilman didn't so much include men in her novel to show the need for unity among the sexes as to show the ridiculousness of male-dominated society. Perhaps this perspective, more than depicting an alternative society, was Gilman's primary goal, and it is one she accomplishes with a wickedly witty sense of humor. Terry is, at best, a caricature of the typical American man, and, at worst, all too representative of this very mono-dimensional male icon. It is primarily Terry's pride Keyser is referring to when she claims "Gilman uses Swift's satire on human pride in general as a model for her attack on male pride in particular" (31). In a fashion similar to Swift in *Gulliver's Travels*, Keyser says, "Gilman is concerned with the way in which people fail to recognize their own strength, allow themselves to be enslaved, and then pride themselves on their identification with the individuals and institutions that enslave them" (31). But, just as feminists today have argued, Gilman thought men were as enslaved as women, as Van often laments in comparing Terry's view to the Herlanders'. "When Terry said 'Sex,' sex with a very large 'S,' he meant the male sex, naturally; its special values, its profound conviction of being 'the life force,' its cheerful ignoring of the true life process, and its interpretation of the other sex solely from its own point of view," Van says. "I had learned to see these things very differently" (Gilman, 134-135).

Perhaps that which Van views most differently as a result of his Herland experience are history and education, often asserted by feminists to be patriarchy's primary means of perpetuating patriarchy. "We boast a good deal of our 'high level of general intelligence' and our 'compulsory public education,' but in proportion to their opportunities they were far better educated than our people," says Van, for "what one knew, all knew" (64-65).

This realization seems especially relevant today in light of E.D. Hirsch's and Allan Bloom's recent attacks on American education as contributing to, rather than solving, the illiteracy problem of contemporary society. Perhaps, however, the problem is not so much what is or isn't taught, but how it is taught. Herlanders, according to Van, "had had no wars. They had had no kings, and no priests, and no aristocracies. They were sisters, and as they grew, they grew together--not by competition, but by united action" (60).

In this fashion, they lived and learned in the present, rather than always in the past--the very place Bloom laments no longer exists, nostalgically longing for the good old days of academic elitism whose demise he boldly asserts feminism was instrumental in causing by being "an enemy of the vitality of classic texts" (64). Indeed, Herlanders have no need or use for history, which amazes Van. "Have you no respect for the past?" he asks Ellador, "for what was thought and believed by your foremothers?"

"Why no," Ellador answers. "Why should we? They are all gone. They knew less than we do. If we are not beyond them, we are unworthy of them--and unworthy of the children who must go beyond us" (Gilman 111).

While Bloom laments that education today is not worthy of its ancestors, Herlanders believe the only importance of education is to be worthy of the future--a future that is here and now rather than, as patriarchal religion believes, exists eternally in an afterlife. "What I cannot understand," says Ellador, "is your preservation of such a very ancient state of mind" (113). The state of mind to which Ellador refers is one that constantly harkens back to God and forward to God, but which seldom provides a way in which to deal with God in the present tense. Herlanders, however, had a "clear established connection between everything they did--and God. Their cleanliness, their health, their exquisite order, the rich peaceful beauty of the whole land, the happiness of the children, and above all the constant progress they made--all this was their religion. They lived as if God was real and at work within them" (115). Overwhelmed, Van can only make the obvious comparison, saying, "You do love one another--you do bear one another's burdens-- you do realize that a little child is a type of the kingdom of heaven. You are more Christian than any people I ever saw" (115).

In the end, Herland offers us via Van, via Gilman, more than patriarchy cares to admit, because it offers an alternative that is not an alternative in the usual sense of being different from, and thereby "less than." *Herland* is relentless in pointing out patriarchy's flaws, so much so, that it is no small wonder that anyone, especially women, can read it and not ask, "Why, having been shown the illogical and oppressive beliefs upon which patriarchy is based, does it not change?" If we are indeed, "we the people," who, "in order to create a more perfect union, establish justice," why is it we still exist in an unjust society and, in fact, an unjust world?

Had we moved forward with the same conscientiousness of Herlanders, we would not need Gilman's book to remind us that seventy-two years later, even though we have survived four wars, gone from wireless radio to satellite television, and watched a man walk on the moon (who, not surprisingly, called the event "one small step for man, one giant leap for mankind"), women are still perceived the way Simone De Beauvoir described them in 1949 as "the second sex." Ultimately, it is with a great amount of sadness, rather than vengeance or spite, that feminists, or, as Gilman would say, humanists should reclaim not only *Herland* as literature, but as a political theory, a more holistic way in which to view the world. With sadness, because in reclaiming not only the book, but the essence of Herland itself, we are not renewing an idea once had and lost, but rather, an idea that has never been. As Ellador asks of Van, "Of course, in a bi-sexual race the distinctive feature of each sex must be intensified. But surely there are characteristics enough which belong to People, aren't there?" (89). In the same way, so must we ask ourselves if there are not enough common characteristics between the sexes to consider ourselves one people in which all are equal, rather than two peoples in which one group is always dominant. In the end, it is not Herland or Hisland that Gilman advocates, but rather, Ourland.

WORKS CITED

Bloom, Allan. *The Closing of the American Mind*. New York: Simon and Schuster, 1987.

Gilman, Charlotte Perkins. *Herland*. New York: Pantheon Books, 1979.

Hill, Mary A. "Charlotte Perkins Gilman: A Feminist's Struggle with Womanhood." *Massachusetts Review* (Fall 1980): 503-526.

Keyser, Elizabeth. "Looking Backward: From *Herland* to *Gulliver's Travels*." *Studies in American Fiction* (Spring 1983): 31-46.

Lane, Ann. Introduction. *Herland*. By Charlotte Perkins Gilman. New York: Pantheon Books, 1979.

Magner, Lois N. "Women and the Scientific Idiom: Textual Episodes from Wollstonecraft, Fuller, Gilman, and Firestone." *Signs* (Autumn 1978): 61-80.

Treichler, Paula A. "Escaping the Sentence: Diagnosis and Discourse in 'The Yellow Wallpaper.'" *Tulsa Studies in Women's Literature* (Spring/Fall 1984): 61-77.

Point/Counterpoint: Considering Opposing Arguments

1. Return to your textbook and review the discussion in Chapter 11 of how to write a research paper. How would you compare and contrast this approach with the method of annotating discussed in your workbook? What value do you find in each approach? Which one do you prefer and why?

2. Has reading Chapter 11 on research papers in both your textbook and your workbook changed any of your initial views of research papers that you expressed in Free Writings #1 and #2? If so, what views have changed and why do you think this change has occurred? If not, which ideas would you present to counter the concepts and viewpoints presented by your textbook and workbook?

3. Of the sample research papers presented in this chapter, which paper do you find the most effective and the most engaging? Why might that be? The styles of these four papers differ; which did you find the most effective and why?

4. Melissa has completed her workbook exercises on the research paper. She turns to you and says, "No matter what this book and my textbook say, I still think writing a research paper is an artificial exercise. It's too contrived, too formulaic, and too uninteresting to me."
How would you respond to Melissa's comments?

5. Virginia agrees with Melissa. "It is not the natural way that people write. And besides, have you ever read an interesting research paper? If research papers are supposed to be such a big deal and teach us so much about writing, why are they all so boring?"
How would you respond to Virginia's views?

6. Phillip responds to Virginia by saying, "I don't like research papers because they rob me of my personal voice. I don't want to write and sound like a textbook or a journal article. I want to sound like *me*. Besides, I think it's ironic that the textbook and the workbook have spent so much time emphasizing the personal voice in writing and how important it is, and then taking away that voice and de-emphasizing it for these research papers? It all seems a huge and unfair contradiction to me."
How would you respond to Phillip?

7. Martin says, "The problem for me is that I like the kind of writing that shakes up the world and makes people open their eyes and think. I don't

think research papers do that. If anything, they seem, to me, like dreary exercises in a lot of busy work associated with library searches and making out 3 x 5 note cards. Who cares about this type of writing, and what practical effect does it have on any one?"

How would you respond to Martin's views?

SUMMARY AND ASSESSMENT PAGE

What ideas from *CHAPTER ELEVEN: WRITING A RESEARCH PAPER* (in either your textbook or your workbook) helped you the most with your writing? What ideas or techniques did you hope to get from this chapter but did not? What steps do you intend to take to learn those ideas or techniques?